# creative
## ACTIVITIES FOR
# Plot, Character & Setting

TERESA GRAINGER
KATHY GOOUCH &
ANDREW LAMBIRTH

**AGES 7-9**

**Authors**
Teresa Grainger,
Kathy Goouch and
Andrew Lambirth

**Editor**
Roanne Charles

**Assistant Editor**
Margaret Eaton

**Series Designers**
Anthony Long and
Joy Monkhouse

**Designer**
Erik Ivens

**Illustrations**
Janet Rogers

**The publishers would like to thank:**

The staff and pupils at **Hextable Infant School**, **Hextable Junior School** and **The Ferncumbe Primary School**.

**Andersen Press Limited** for the use of an extract from *Mr Bear and the Bear* by Frances Thomas © 1994, Frances Thomas (1994, Andersen Press Ltd).

**DC Thomson and Co Ltd** for the use of characters and front covers of *The Beano* and *The Dandy* © DC Thomson and Co Ltd. www.beanotown.com, www.dandy.com.

**The authors would like to thank** all the energetic and creative professionals on the Advanced Certificate in Creativity in Literacy Learning, and the Masters courses in Language and Literacy who have trialled these ideas in their classrooms; all the talented children who supplied work included in this publication.

**Published by Scholastic Ltd,
Villiers House,
Clarendon Avenue,
Leamington Spa,
Warwickshire CV32 5PR**

www.scholastic.co.uk

Text © 2004 Teresa Grainger, Kathy Goouch and Andrew Lambirth
© 2004 Scholastic Ltd

Designed using Adobe Indesign

Printed by Belmont Press, Northampton

2 3 4 5 6 7 8 9   4 5 6 7 8 9 0 1 2 3

**British Library Cataloguing-in-Publication Data**

A catalogue record for this book is available from the British Library.

ISBN 0-439-97112-8

The rights of Teresa Grainger, Kathy Goouch and Andrew Lambirth to be identified as the Authors of this work have been asserted by them in accordance with the Copyright, Designs and Patents Act 1988.

# Contents

# Introduction

Stories play a significant role in children's development as readers, writers and tellers of tales. Opportunities abound in school for children to engage with powerful fiction, to enter the imaginary worlds presented and to extend their understanding of the choices writers have made. Between the ages of seven and nine, children begin to embed their knowledge of how narrative works and become more aware of the various elements of stories, such as character, setting plot, theme and language. In the process, they explore many texts and begin to notice and make use of these aspects of story grammar, all of which are focused upon in the National Curriculum and the National Literacy Strategy.

Five years after the implementation of the Literacy Strategy in England, many primary teachers have begun to flex their professional muscles, exercise their informed judgement and make full use of their years of experience in this area of learning. Despite the pressures of accountability and prescription, indeed perhaps because of them, teachers are becoming aware that to be effective the literacy curriculum needs a more creative approach. Such an approach acknowledges the importance of knowledge about language, but highlights the creative application of such knowledge. Recently, naming and knowing seem to have been profiled at the expense of engaging with language and creatively using language. 'My Year 3s all know what a suffix is,' a friend has confided, 'but they don't like writing and never choose to write – so what's the point?' Achieving a balance between knowledge about language, which can be measured and tested, and creative use of language is essential if we are to motivate and involve our young learners.

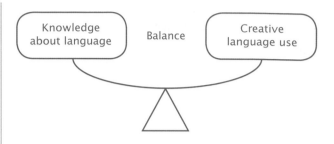

*The balancing act of literacy teaching*

Children do need to develop knowledge about language, and should be supported in making their implicit knowledge explicit. However, the development of such knowledge and understanding must be offered in a manner that invites creative engagement and flexibility, and encourages the voice of the writer and the views and interest of the reader. A much more effective balance needs to be created in classrooms between form and freedom, accuracy and fluency, structure and innovation in literacy learning.

## Creative literacy learning

'The more prescriptive the curriculum, the greater the need to be explicit about creativity and not leave it to chance.' The Design Council, quoted in *All Our Futures, Creativity, Culture and the Curriculum* (DfEE).

The series *Creative Activities for Plot, Character and Setting* focuses on teaching story elements imaginatively across the primary years. All three of the books (also for ages 5–7 and 9–11) respond to the requirements of national curricula as well as the recommendations in the National Literacy Strategy in a creative and flexible manner. The books are based on the belief that effective teachers of literacy are informed and creative teachers of literacy, teachers who build strong relationships, know about language and learning and are both responsive to learners' needs and able to inspire and motivate them to ensure deep learning. Such teachers create imaginative contexts for purposeful literacy use and thoughtfully play their way forwards, making full use of open-ended literacy activities, as well as employing direct instruction when appropriate.

The wealth of interactive activities offered in this book is intended to support teachers in developing more exploratory approaches to narrative. There are no formulae here, no panaceas, but a bias towards the innovative is evident, and playfulness and imaginative engagement are actively encouraged. In enabling children to explore stories 'from the inside out', and to journey into the unknown with their teacher, the activities celebrate the critical role of creativity in the process of literacy learning.

Teachers are invited to experiment with the activities, and to take a full part in them, responding to their learners and adapting the ideas flexibly. Many of the activities in *Creative Activities for Plot, Character and Setting* for ages 5–7 or 9–11 can be adapted or used immediately with children aged 7–9 years. In adopting more creative approaches, both teachers and children will be involved in the generation of ideas and the evaluation of them, and will enrich their understanding of narrative elements in the process.

## The range of possible narratives

Children of this age will be meeting a range of narratives at home: through conversations, television, cinema, DVD, in graphic novels, electronic media and comics. The books they encounter in school – whether picture fiction or short novels – will need to be high-quality examples of the best available and need to be enriched by examples from other forms too (such as films and comics). The genres of fiction listed in the National Literacy Strategy for this age group include: stories with familiar settings, adventure stories, stories by the same author, adventure and mystery stories, stories from other cultures, historical stories, stories about imaginary worlds, stories that raise issues and traditional tales of all kinds (myths, legends, fables and parables). Almost any text a teacher wanted to share with her class across this time could therefore be fitted into this encompassing brief. This is important, as teachers need to feel free to choose books they know and like and believe will work for their class.

Knowledge of books is central to the practical strategies offered here, as only certain stories will, for example, support the development of an emotion graph or a name game. Generally, however, the activities can be applied to any text. Picture fiction and traditional tales are likely to be the easiest and most effective to use. In high-quality picture books and in retold traditional tales from many cultures, the narrative elements are frequently more overtly signalled and therefore easier for the class to notice, to engage with and to emulate. In novels, the complexity of the plot and the gradual development of the subtle tendencies of a key character can make the challenge more difficult for young learners. In addition, multi-modal texts, such as picture books or oral stories, which use more than one mode to communicate their meaning, are the norm in children's worlds and need to be given space in the classroom. Most significantly, however, teachers expect children to write short stories and so need to read and study short stories in picture books and anthologies as these provide more suitable models than long novels.

With each activity in the book, suggestions are made for literature links. These encompass texts suitable for study at this age and suitable for the activity, they prioritise picture fiction and traditional tales but frequently include modern short stories and novels. This bias towards traditional folklore and picture fiction is in response to the need to identify examples from which children can emulate and learn about narrative elements most easily. You will know many other books and videos that suit a particular activity and engage your learners. To honour the text and the children's interests, tailored text extracts read out of context must be avoided. However, with the wealth of children's picture fiction and novels available, extracts from the book being read as a class or from films being watched can easily be found and used. A narrative needs to be both powerful and enticing to support the motivated involvement and imaginative engagement of the children.

## Integrating reading, writing and speaking and listening

The significance of all three language modes operating in harmony together needs to be recognised and can be made a working reality in the classroom. Teachers know that children need time to talk about texts, to make sense of them, and that talking before, during and after writing can help young writers communicate more effectively. Yet with so many detailed teaching objectives to cover, and in response to the pressure of written tests, talk is often short-changed. The number of teaching objectives in Year 3 of the National Literacy Strategy rises exponentially from Year 2, and 90 per cent of this is at word and sentence level. This may mean that an overemphasis on these technical aspects of literacy develops at this age. If teachers are not very careful, this could be at the expense of developing children's text-level understanding and engagement with the world of a story.

Teacher Training Agency research has shown that effective teachers of literacy profile the meanings of stories and contextualise the teaching of word-, text- and sentence-level skills in powerful narratives that appeal to the children (*Effective Teachers of Literacy* by Wray and Medwell, Routledge). The activities suggested therefore need to be integrated into related units of work, since they cannot on their own enable richer learning about narrative elements. In a unit of work on traditional tales, for example, the stories retold here could be used and several of the activities employed across the three- or four-week block to involve the children imaginatively and support their understanding of one or more narrative elements. The National Literacy Strategy text-level objectives for these years in relation to reading and writing narrative cover the full range of narrative elements, including settings and the vocabulary of story language, a focus on themes in each year as well as story structure and characters. Seven- to nine-year-olds are expected to develop their awareness of how these features relate to one another – for example, how setting influences narrative action and how characters' actions can be predicted.

The objectives in the new guidelines *Speaking, Listening, Learning: working with children* are also addressed in the activities, with plenty of opportunities for speaking and listening to one another in pairs, small group discussion of texts and a range of drama activities to bring a text to life. Talk is woven through all the narrative activities suggested, many of which suit shared reading or writing and can be used as support for independent reading and writing. Some describe, for example, a reading-focused activity, although writing possibilities may emerge as the activity is undertaken. Development possibilities are also offered, which you can select from and then shape and transform in interaction with the children. The book aims to support the imaginative teaching of narrative elements, enabling the children to learn through their creative involvement with the meaning of the text.

# Chapter One

# Story Structure

**Story structures can be examined, discussed, experienced and composed in the classroom. In order to notice the structure of certain narratives, their structural similarity to other tales and the overall shape of narratives, children need to enjoy and engage with well-structured stories.**

Short stories in which the development and structure of the narrative is particularly clear can operate as explicit models for children's own narrative writing. Children need to hear such narratives read aloud and work in exploratory contexts that represent the structure in a variety of ways. This may involve them in drawing, talking, improvising, and re-creating scenes both symbolically and literally. They also need to actively voice stories and retell tales in order to experience the verbal patterning and felt experience of the narrative. Story maps, story mountains and freeze-frames (see pages 14, 18 and 22) can all be used to represent the structure, but this can only be internalised through the practice of oral storytelling and through a wide engagement with literature.

The National Literacy Strategy profiles various aspects of narrative structure for children aged 7–9, and 12 specific reading and writing objectives are included across the two years, which focus on this. The bias is heavily towards planning story writing. It is clear, however, that shared reading activities, such as examining well-known texts or oral stories, are needed to support writing objectives like plotting episodes of a story or planning a story to identify the stages of its telling. The spoken word plays a critical role in the learning process as children deconstruct one tale in order to construct a new one. Oral work can help children understand and experience the structure of tales as they are voiced or shown in sequenced improvisations.

The use of literary models is particularly important in supporting children's awareness of story structure; varied openings and alternative endings can be examined, temporal connectives can be taught in context; build-ups and conflicts can be identified; various story structures can be explored with the class, and teachers can list over time other narratives which follow similar plot patterns. Examples of these are listed below, including tales on problem resolution, journeys, cumulative tales, days of the week and climactic tales, to mention but a few.

A particular story structure can be a useful focus for a unit of work, using displays of texts with the given structure and providing the opportunity for children to hear, read, tell and write tales with a similar structure.

## Problem-resolution tales

These often reflect a clear difficulty at the start of the narrative; then a series of steps are taken by the protagonist to resolve this difficulty. The problem is finally resolved, often by ingenious means, at the close of the tale. The activity 'Zipped books' (page 10) can be helpful to prompt exploration of problem-resolution tales, if the difficulty or challenge to the characters is not explicit in the title. Picture books and novels in this category include:

- ***The Cat That Scratched*** and ***The Dog That Dug*** – Jonathan Long (Red Fox)
- ***The Boy and the Cloth of Dreams*** – Jenny Koralek (Walker Books)
- ***The Owl Who Was Afraid of the Dark*** – Jill Tomlinson (Egmont)
- ***Red Eyes at Night*** – Michael Morpurgo (Hodder Children's Books)
- ***Loudmouth Louis*** – Anne Fine (Puffin).

## Journey tales

These stories often involve the main character in meeting a series of people, animals or places on his/her journey. Sometimes s/he returns home enriched by the experience, in other stories s/he remains in the new setting (one-way journeys, A to B). The narrative order varies, but often encompasses a variation on: introduction – build up – climaxes or conflicts – resolutions. The activity 'Story mountains' (page 14) is useful in mapping out the structure of climactic tales. Return journey stories (travel from A to B to A) include the following books and stories:

- ***The House Cat*** – Helen Cooper (Scholastic)
- ***Sleeping Nanna*** – Kevin Crossley-Holland (Orchard)
- **'Little River Turtle'** (a traditional tale in this book – see page 88)
- ***The Rainbow Bear*** – Michael Morpurgo (Corgi)
- ***The Thistle Princess and Other Stories*** – Vivian French (Walker Books)
- ***Emma's Doll*** – Brian Patten (Puffin).

One-way journey stories (from A to B) include the following:

- **On the Way Home** – Jill Murphy (Macmillan)
- **Going West** – Martin Waddell (Puffin)
- **The Little Boat** – Kathy Henderson (Walker Books)
- **'The Willow Pattern Story'** (page 84).

## Cumulative tales

These tales include a series of events or the introduction of characters at regular intervals as the narrative grows cumulatively. Towards the close of the narrative, something happens to explode the situation or to drastically change the status quo. The activity 'Cumulative story graphs' (page 16) is helpful in examining such tales. Examples of stories which are cumulative in nature are:

- **'The Tailor's Button'** (a traditional tale on page 86)
- **'There Was an Old Woman Who Swallowed a Fly'** (a traditional tale)
- **'The Enormous Turnip'** (a traditional tale)
- **Handa's Surprise** – Eileen Browne (Walker Books)

- **'There's Some Sky in this Pie'** in **A Necklace of Raindrops and Other Stories** – Joan Aiken (Yearling).

## Climactic tales

In these tales the narrative builds to a marked crescendo and an often explosive climax after which the characters may return home or the tale ends. Stories that are climactic in nature include:

- **Giant** – Juliet Snape (Walker Books)
- **The Rascally Cake** – Jeanne Willis (Puffin)
- **Angus Rides the Goods Train** – Alan Durant (Corgi)
- **Little Tim and the Brave Sea Captain** – Edward Ardizzone (Scholastic).

**The activities in this chapter seek to bring narrative structures to life, to help children notice the construction of the plot and to identify the key incidents and sequenced stages of a tale's telling. This will enrich their reading and be used as a mirror for their writing.**

# Zipped books

**This activity encourages children to generate their own stories based on the visuals on picture book covers. The children's initial ideas can then be shaped and honed by producing a story map of the imagined tale's structure, which may itself lead to writing the predicted narrative, or some part of it. In effect, a tale is hypothesised in pairs and a coherent story plan is produced. The books themselves will not initially be read, so look out for enticing pictures on covers, which hint at the narrative but do not create a résumé of the story inside.**

## What to do

❶ Select 10 to 15 quality picture books that are likely to be unknown to the children.

❷ Imaginatively explain that there is something remarkable about these books: they are zipped up tight. Demonstrate with one that there is an invisible zip (visible only to those with imagination) along the three non-spine sides of the book and therefore the book cannot be easily opened. Depending on your class, you could suggest these zips are magical and woven by fairies, or part of a new publishing gimmick and so on. You might explain that if a zip is broken, somewhere a fairy will lose the capacity to fly, or the publishers will recall the books or charge double! Whatever scenario you create, the idea is to creatively entice the children into the activity. You may want to put the books in plastic zip-bags or sealed clear wallets to prevent opening.

❸ Explain that you will offer each pair or group of three children a few books and that they need to select one book between them. Stress that they should choose one that they don't know already but are tempted to explore. Remind them that they can read the text and the visuals on the front and back of the book to help them, including any blurb that is available. These may provoke rich ideas and possibilities.

❹ Suggest that the pairs create the story of their zipped book, and offer them a series of questions to get them going. For

## Literature links

High-quality picture books suit this activity, particularly those without a synopsis or significant blurb on the back cover. The book needs to be unknown to the pair predicting from it. Suggested examples are:

● *Going West* – Martin Waddell (Puffin)
● *The Yellow Train* – Alistair Highet (Creative Editions)
● *The White Crane* – Junko Morimoto (Collins)
● *The House Cat* – Helen Cooper (Scholastic)
● *Cloudland* – John Burningham (Red Fox)
● *The Sea of Tranquility* – Mark Haddon (Picture Lions).

example, *What might happen? Is there a central problem that needs to be resolved? What steps might the main character take to resolve this situation?* Or, *Who do you think is the main character? What might he or she do at the beginning, the middle and the end?* Allow plenty of time for ideas to be generated. You may wish to let the children start talking on their own initiative, then intervene after five minutes or so with these shaping questions to help the discussion progress.

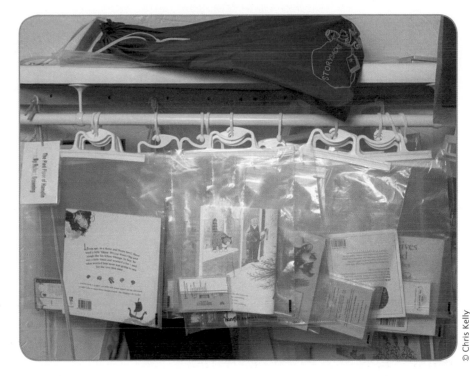

© Chris Kelly

⑤ Give the children at least five more minutes, then interrupt the conversation, explaining that shortly they will have the chance to tell their tale to another pair. This will help focus their predictions and will enable the story structure to develop, providing you make it clear to the children they will not be telling new partners *about* the book but will be telling the story.

⑥ Organise the children into fours, letting pairs tell their zipped-book narrative to each other. This will help the children to fix their story in their minds.

⑦ Now provide time for pairs to collaboratively map out their story structure in some way, for example using pictograms, symbols, a skeleton, a story hand or key words. All of these are simple ways to represent the key elements in the story: using the backbone of the skeleton or the digits in a drawing of a hand.

⑧ You could close this activity with the children writing their tales in full, or pairs could select a paragraph from their plan to flesh out in detail.

⑨ Now give the pairs the chance to unzip and read their chosen book, to discuss it and reflect upon comparisons with their own story.

## Moving on

● Extend the discussion to encompass the focus on a main character: what his or her name might be, what key actions she might take, what she learns during the story. One or two key characters are often included in the cover illustration and this can help children create a relationship between central characters and the structure of their story.

● You could put off sharing the books for several weeks, until the children's own stories have been written. This should sustain and build the children's interest in the zipped books. Then, ask the school secretary or caretaker to deliver the 'keys' to unlock the zips, and allow pairs of children the privilege of reading their unzipped book. Displays, 'compare and contrast' charts, story maps, and letters to the author or illustrator may then emerge from this.

# Story plates

This activity provides children with an imaginative visual approach that will help them record the main events and sequence key incidents of a narrative. Using the model provided by the famous willow pattern plate (see the story on page 84), children are encouraged to illustrate a story plate of their own that describes and sequences the main points in a story. The story could be their own choice or one you have told or read. The story plate can then be used to support the children's retelling of the tale to others, which in turn will help to embed the pattern of the tale in their story memory. Later, the story plate activity can be used to plan the main points of a story, forming a structure for narrative writing.

## Literature links

This activity works best with obviously structured stories, for example traditional tales like 'There Was an Old Woman Who Swallowed a Fly' and 'The Tailor's Button' (see page 86), or *Mrs Armitage on Wheels* by Quentin Blake (Red Fox), a tale from *A Web of Stories* by Grace Hallworth (Mammoth) or *Hairy Toes and Scary Bones* by Rose Impey (Orchard).

## What to do

❶ Read the story of the willow pattern plate (see page 84).

❷ As a shared activity, identify and sequence the key incidents:

The daughter (Koong-Se) of a rich mandarin (an important official) falls in love with a poor servant (Chang); they meet secretly, but are eventually discovered. She is imprisoned behind a high wall, betrothed to an old ta-jin (a nobleman) she doesn't even know, and is to marry him *when the peach tree blossoms in the spring*. The lovers still send messages to each other, while the ta-jin sends pre-wedding gifts to the mandarin. One night, when the mandarin, ta-jin and servants are drunk, Chang and Koong-Se run away with the jewels. Although chased by Koong-Se's father and servants, they manage to escape and marry. They are found, but again manage to escape to a tiny island. They sell the jewels to build a home and Chang writes a book. The book leads the ta-jin to Chang. He kills him, and the despairing Koong-Se sets fire to the house and is burned to death. The gods turn the lovers into a pair of doves.

Willow Pattern plate kindly loaned by Mortimer's Curios of Leamington Spa

③ Show the children a willow pattern plate (or a picture of one) and examine it to identify the images. There are no rights and wrongs here about what the pictures show; indeed the numerous retellings testify to the various ways in which the plate's images have been interpreted over time. However, the children will be able to see the various elements of the story, such as the high wall which imprisoned Koong-Se and separated the lovers, the willow tree, the bridge (with arguably the three figures of the mandarin, Koong-Se and Chang), the home the lovers built on the island, and the two doves circling in the sky. Discuss how the design of the plate's decoration reflects the significant events in the narrative in a reasonably chronological sequence. Consider with the children other ways in which the tale might have been depicted. For example, through simpler symbolic pictures; by sectioning the plate; by presenting pictures in a spiral from the outside inwards.

④ Ask the class to select a traditional tale (or a chapter from the longer story you are reading, or your shared reading text) on which they can base their own story plate design using a paper plate. This activity will work best if the first time you do it all the children make a story plate of the same narrative. You could make good use of one of the stories in this book, for example 'The Tailor's Button' (page 86) or 'Anansi and Postman Snake' (page 94).

⑤ Allow the children some time to discuss key elements of the plot with writing partners, before completing a rough plan of their design on a circle of paper. Then let them create their story pattern on a paper plate.

⑥ Share the different ways the children have tackled this presentation, for example, as a sequence of pictures, from a character's point of view, symbolic representation, various divisions of the circle.

⑦ If different stories have been used, let the children to use their plates as a memory prompt when retelling their tale (or parts of it) to a partner, or allow them to select their favourite part to retell.

## Moving on

● Consider encouraging the children to take their story plates home to tell their tales to family members.

● Plan a storytelling afternoon in which the children become storytellers for another class (for example in the hall), making full use of their story plates. On such an occasion, bright cloths or shawls draped over chairs will give status to the storytellers who can show their plates as they tell their tales, in pairs if appropriate.

# Story mountains

This activity uses the varied shapes and sizes of a mountain range to act as a visual representation of a story structure. It works well with climactic stories and enables children to deconstruct the key events in a story and consider how the narrative has been ordered. Once the structure is clear, new tales can be created based on the same mountain 'formation', with perhaps a series of three or four significant events (three mountain peaks). In this way, a new tale is built on the organisational features of an existing one. The overall mountain-range shape can show the high points and low points in the narrative (in terms of excitement, drama, danger and so on), and help children to see links between key sections.

## Literature links

Many traditional tales have clear structures that suit this mountain range activity. The picture books *Chinye* by Obi Onyefulu (Frances Lincoln), *How Night Came* by Joanna Troughton (Puffin) and *Abiyoyo* by Pete Seeger (Atheneum) would be good to use, and there are others based on a climactic structure, such as *Angus Rides the Goods Train* by Alan Durant (Corgi). The simple tales *What Made Tiddalik Laugh* by Joanna Troughton (Puffin) and *Handa's Surprise* by Eileen Browne (Walker) are also useful for story mountains, as they have regular repeating patterns.

## What to do

❶ Tell or read a highly structured tale, such as 'Little River Turtle' (page 88), or another patterned traditional tale or text.

❷ Introduce the idea of the narrative having a certain shape, for example the flattish opening, the build-up, high point(s) of a climax or series of climaxes and lower levels of temporary or final resolutions.

❸ In shared writing, record the key events of the tale as words that form mountain outlines, letting the build-up be shown as a rise; the series of events in the middle of the narrative as mountain peaks, and the resolution as the story descending.

(See the example outlined in point 4 below which indicates this rise and fall as well as the significant narrative elements in the middle of the story.)

© Chris Kelly

④ Show the class a sugar paper or card mountain range you have cut already, based on another well-known tale, such as 'The Three Little Pigs'. The flat land at the side of the mountain range will be represented by them leaving home; then there will be three clear peaks – one for each of the pigs as the wolf comes to blow their houses down. The final descent of the tale and last piece of flat land may be represented by the pigs defeating the wolf and living happily ever after.

⑤ Decide with the class what shape to make a mountain range that reflects the structure of the story you are using. Agree a shape together and draw this on the board so the children can copy it.

⑥ Invite the children to cut out their own story mountains and then draw simple pictures to represent the narrative events in the mountain's structure.

⑦ Explain to the children that they are going to be storytellers for another class. Encourage groups to practise retelling their story, dividing up the narrative or taking parts and making use of a narrator.

⑧ Visit another class, sit your group on storytellers' chairs (covered with cloths, shawls and so on) and allow them time to retell their tale. A simple chant at the beginning and end, for example *Crick Crack Chin Our Story's In and Crick Crack Snout Our Story's Out*, will help create traditional boundaries for the telling.

## Moving on

● Use the same idea to help children plan their own stories, cutting out different mountain ranges and mapping key elements in the narrative. Allow time to retell a chosen part of this tale. In shared writing, model how to move from simple pictures into paragraphs for the mountains and the slopes introducing and concluding the tale.

● Repeat the activity with a range of tales. The children's versions may well be different from how you would have created them, but providing they can retell the tale and have included the key elements, do not worry; their use of this visual support will be refined with experience.

● Encourage the children to devise alternative narrative shapes related to particular stories – for example, a bundle of matches for Hans Christian Andersen's *The Little Match Girl* or dancing shoes for the Grimms' *The Twelve Dancing Princesses*. The important feature is that the narrative structure can be reflected in the shape. For example, the Little Match Girl looks through three windows so, including these events with the beginning and the end, only five matches will be needed. However, as with all creative activities, hard and fast rules are not appropriate and the children may well be able to defend their innovative ideas – in which case, celebrate them!

● Plan a storytelling afternoon with your class and encourage the children to select a tale to tell (not a well-known one). Preparation time will need to be set aside for this. Individuals could choose whether to do a story plate, a storyboard or a story mountain to support their retelling and aid recall. Parents could be invited and perhaps a visiting storyteller as well: contact the Society for Storytelling (0118 935 1381; www.sfs.org.uk).

# Cumulative story graphs

This activity suits cumulative tales in which events or characters are repeatedly added to the unfolding narrative until an often explosive climax is reached. To help children appreciate the structural patterns inherent in such tales, block graphs can be used. Many cumulative tales, whilst regular in manner and in their repetitive language patterns, can be extremely flexible in retelling. For example, in 'The Tailor's Button' (page 86) in which the tailor makes progressively smaller items of clothing, the exact order of garments doesn't necessarily matter, providing of course they all diminish in size. However, by committing the structure to a graph, this can be discussed and the graph used as a prompt for retelling. Children can also design their own graphs to map out new cumulative tales that are easy to achieve, visually attractive and creatively engaging.

## What to do

❶ Read or tell a cumulative story, prompting the class to join in with appropriate actions, for example the snipping, stitching and sewing in 'The Tailor's Button'. These actions serve to highlight the repeating patterns in the tale.

❷ Discuss the accumulating characters or, in the case of 'The Tailor's Button', the increasing variety but decreasing size of the pieces of clothing the tailor makes. For example, he begins with a jacket and when the cloth begins to wear at the elbows, he makes himself a waistcoat, and later a cravat, and so on.

❸ Discuss any further features of the tale together, such as the tailor's confidence which grows every time he wears a new garment, however small, made out of the precious material.

## Literature links

A number of traditional tales are cumulative in nature, such as 'The Enormous Turnip'. 'There Was an Old Woman Who Swallowed a Fly', the folk tale 'The Tailor's Button' (see page 86) and *The Do-it-yourself House that Jack Built* by Quentin Blake (Puffin) are also cumulative in manner. In addition, simple block graphs can be undertaken with stories that follow the days of the week, for example *Jasper's Beanstalk* by Nick Butterworth and Mick Inkpen (Hodder Children's Books), *The Very Hungry Caterpillar* by Eric Carle (Puffin) and *Mr Wolf's Week* by Colin and Jacqui Hawkins (Egmont). Whilst the last three are simply structured and not particularly challenging texts for this age range, they are excellent examples for children to lean upon because the structure is clear and can be imitated with ease.

❹ Retell the first part of the tale together; then stop and draw the first part of the cumulative graph (see below), inviting the children to suggest what simple symbols or visuals you might draw in the first two or three boxes.

❺ As you continue the story, add to the graph so that as a class you have constructed a nearly complete cumulative story graph of 'The Tailor's Button'. Encourage the class to join in with the repetitive story language, as this highlights and marks the structure. In 'The Tailor's Button', the choral refrains are clear: *So, by candlelight, he snipped and he clipped, he snipped and he clipped, and he stitched and he sewed, he stitched and he sewed until he'd fashioned himself a ___; and Whenever the tailor wore his ___, he felt goood about himself; so very goood about himself in fact that he...*

❻ Discuss the use of a chorus like this and its role in making clear to the reader or listener that the next stage of the story has begun. You might even want to mark on the graph the placement of the first chorus (with a picture of a small pair of scissors, for example), which will show the regularity of the refrain and indicate the diminishing, but heavily structured, nature of the frame.

❼ Invite the children to draw their own block graphs, completing the one begun in shared work, or for another cumulative tale, such as 'There Was an Old Woman Who Swallowed a Fly'. Let them choose which to work upon.

❽ Show the children how each bar of the graph can represent a paragraph in the tale and ask them to rewrite one or two paragraphs using their story graphs as a

basis to work from. Focus also on connecting phrases so there is cohesion even across two paragraphs, and remind the children that the memorable story language of the chorus will need to repeat fairly consistently. This does, however, make the task of writing out those parts of the tale easier!

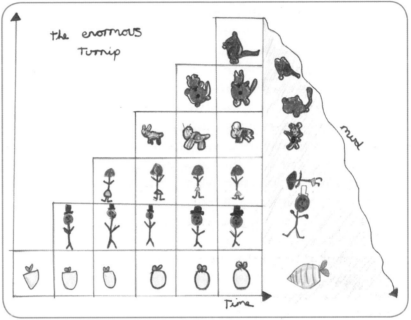

## Moving on

● Invent together a range of accompanying actions for the class retelling of the tale. These will aid recall and help the children to notice the regularity of the choral chant and its role in shaping the narrative.

● Focus explicitly on patterned language and work to write alternative versions of a story that uses repetitive language for the same purpose – demarcating the episodic and cumulative structure of the tale.

● The children could use graphs to plan their own narratives in a similar manner, for example 'The Seamstress's Button', 'There Was a Schoolteacher Who Swallowed a Rubber', 'The Demon Headmaster's Outing' and so on. Modelling one and writing a class graph together can be good fun; then you could challenge the children to work collaboratively to produce their own.

# Story maps

This activity can be used to help children understand and record the main events in a story and to sequence those events. It also encourages children to develop a personal response to a story, and come to understand this response, as they recall events, characters and emotions that they perceive as the most significant in the story. This experience will feed into their exploration of theme when they undertake the activities described in Chapter 4. Children can use a picture map like this to retell a story to an audience, with the recorded elements of their map acting as a supporting list of contents. The maps should become a permanent personal resource for individual children, but copies could also be useful as part of a class display.

## Literature links

Story maps can be created for any fiction text, but for less experienced readers it may be helpful if the narrative is centred around a journey, list or structured chain of events, as these tend to provide the most memorable and easily transferable sequences. Suggested books that can be successfully mapped are:

- *The Cat that Scratched* – Jonathan Long (Red Fox)
- *The House Cat* – Helen Cooper (Scholastic)
- *Sleeping Nanna* – Kevin Crossley-Holland (Orchard)
- *Flat Stanley* – Jeff Brown (Egmont)
- *The Shrinking of Treehorn* – Florence Parry Heide (Puffin)
- *Angus Rides the Goods Train* – Alan Durant (Corgi).

## What to do

1. Begin by reading the whole story if it is a short picture book, or by reading a fairly eventful part of a longer story that you are currently reading with the children.

2. Ask the children to use whiteboards, individually or in pairs, to record very simple line drawings or symbolic images to represent parts of the story that they feel are important, for instance in moving the narrative on.

3. Re-read the story, inviting the children as you do so to redraw their appropriate drawing/symbol on the board so that together you build up a map showing all of the key incidents in the story. This may look like a route map, or a series of events with linking arrows. The format will depend on your chosen story. For example, a story map of *Angus Rides the Goods Train* by Alan Durant would suit the form of a train track. You may need to discuss and negotiate with the children some of these incidents if you have more than one interpretation, or save some to include on either individual maps or an additional class story map if you feel you have too many.

4. When the map is complete, retell the story together as a class, using the simple

pictures to help. During this retelling, it would be helpful if written subtitles of events could be scribed on the board. Modelling this will help the children develop their own maps and oral tellings into written versions. It could also be part of a lively display, incorporating more than one mapped version of the same story.

⑤ Select one aspect of the story to retell in more detail in shared writing, demonstrating how to turn a picture and its subtitle/caption into a brief descriptive or narrative passage which fleshes out that particular moment in the story.

## Moving on

● To extend this activity, encourage the children to add temporal connectives to the map to indicate the time frame of the story, for example *initially, two days later, meanwhile, finally.* This could be done at first with simple annotations on Post-it notes which are positioned next to the appropriate symbols/ sketches on the map.

● Give small groups of children an A3 sheet of paper and fat felt-tipped pens. Ask them to collaborate on the construction of a story map from another text of their choice, or a given text in the genre being explored during a particular unit of work. This will consolidate narrative work done in this activity and encourage group discussion, negotiation and decision-making skills.

© Chris Kelly

# Storytelling

**This activity aims to help children recall the main events in a story narrative, practise their storytelling skills and engage an audience. Ordering and articulating the significant elements in their orally told stories will support children in their written story structures. This practice will also help children develop a sense of purpose and audience for their stories. It would be useful to carry out this activity after children have experienced at least one other story structure activity, for example 'Story plates' (page 12), 'Cumulative story graphs' (page 16) and 'Story maps' (page 18).**

## What to do

❶ Tell the children about the *Jackanory* television series that ran from the 1960s to the 1990s. If possible, show videos of people telling stories during shared reading time or other available opportunities, or discuss storytelling events the children may have been to or seen on television.

© Chris Kelly

## Literature links

To further support children in this activity it is suggested that for their first experiences they are encouraged to lean on traditional tales that are well known to them (for example 'Little Red Riding Hood' or 'The Three Little Pigs'), or stories that have been told to them and retained by them through storytelling activities, such as 'The Tailor's Button' (page 86), 'Little River Turtle' (page 88), 'The Rajah's Big Ears' (page 91) or 'Anansi and Postman Snake' (page 94).

© Ingram Publishing

❷ Discuss the nature and appeal of such programmes and notice any strategies that are used to support the telling, for example full-screen illustrations, a puppet used by the storyteller, a special storytelling chair positioned at the fireside, special clothes or a costume (perhaps a cloak or hat), and so on. This is an opportunity to explore all the non-verbal and visual supports that effective storytellers use, drawing on children's experiences at libraries, storytelling events or from television. Discuss why these strategies are used: for example, to exaggerate humour, to highlight pathos, to help the listener 'see' the characters and settings. Explain that *Jackanory* stories were often told in five episodes across the week, with each episode ending in a cliffhanger to maintain momentum and keep the listener interested.

❸ Over the course of a unit of work (or over a couple of weeks) read, then retell, two or three stories. Explain to the children that they will need to be able to retell a story like this, of their own choice.

④ Before each of your own storytelling sessions, remind the children of ways of recalling events and patterns and the 'tune' of the story they hear (using key words, story maps, story plates etc).

⑤ In addition to these experiences, provide opportunities for the children, in pairs, to share well-known traditional tales such as 'Little Red Riding Hood'. Ask them to take turns to tell and to listen, and support each other in retelling them.

⑥ Give pairs of children time to rehearse a story they have chosen to tell together. Advise them to select one they know well and to use cues from their plates or graphs. Discuss the effect of voice and intonation on the listener and how pauses and changes of pace can influence tension and suspense as well as sustain interest. Model and practise this with the children. They may want to consider other effects and turn off some lights and close curtains or blinds to create an appropriate atmosphere.

⑦ Depending on the age and experience of the children, offer props to support them as they tell their story to the class – perhaps a device such as a cut-out cardboard frame to represent a television screen, or a real microphone.

⑧ Provide the opportunity for their *Jackanory* session to be video- or audio-taped, if possible. This will help the children to critically examine their own performances and each other's.

⑨ Encourage the children to develop a repertoire of tales they can tell in this way, using as few props as possible. Ideally, look to provide opportunities of this nature as a regular activity.

© Derek Cooknell

## Moving on

● As an ongoing activity, you could make the props and a tape recorder available to enable the children to continue rehearsing their storytelling skills and recall of the tunes and patterns of well-structured stories. These rehearsals could be organised in pairs or small groups. More simply, you could include a storytelling session as part of the weekly routine with a special storytelling chair and clothing or other props, which will help to raise the status of the activity.

● Consider encouraging the children to develop their storytelling further by providing them with a larger audience – such as another class, the assembly audience, parents and other visitors, and/or hold a storytelling afternoon.

# Freeze-frames

The focus of this activity is on representing the key events in a short story, picture book or chapter of a novel as a series of still images using the drama technique of freeze-frame or tableau. In effect, a physical storyboard is made. This involves the whole class in taking part in sectioning the story and re-creating the narrative structure. It is a useful shared reading activity that considers the structure of a text and its series of significant scenes. It is also useful as a precursor to shared writing, as the titles/captions of the silent tableaux combine to create a powerful summary of the story. This enables children to retell the main points of the story in sequence. Additionally, the subsequent narrative events in a novel – implied by the chapter titles – can be predicted and made into freeze-frames.

## What to do

❶ Re-read a well-known short story or chapter and ask the children to clap each time another episode in the narrative begins. Some picture books use each double-page spread to reflect the episodic structure; this may be a useful starting point, moving on to more complex narratives when the children are used to the idea.

❷ Each time you stop and a new episode is identified, allocate this episode to a pair or small group of children to form into a tableau. Tell the children to all remain seated until the tale is completed, but to remember their allocation.

❸ Invite the pairs or groups to form themselves into freeze-frames of their episode, representing the key event and

## Literature links

This activity works well with overtly structured picture books and novels with episodic chapters. The series of *This is the Bear* books by Sarah Hayes and Helen Craig (Walker Books) are highly patterned, operating to the formula *This is the... and this is the... who...*, which is helpful to a class new to this type of activity. The stories themselves will not tax Year 3 children, but the focus here is on analysis of narrative structure. Chapters from the novels *Pure Dead Magic* or *Pure Dead Wicked* by Debi Gliori (Doubleday) are action-packed and would suit demonstrating a sequence of narrative incidents. Alternatively, the chapter titles can be used to make a series of freeze-frames that represent the whole text. *Rats!* by Pat Hutchins (Red Fox) and *Clive and the Missing Finger* by Sarah Garland (Puffin) particularly suit freeze-frames in this way. The traditional tales retold at the back of this book would also suit freeze-frames of narrative action.

clearly showing the characters' dispositions. Make sure the children have a little time to discuss, practise, create and amend these silent tableaux.

④ Re-read or retell the whole tale, with each group showing their tableau in sequence to form the narrative.

⑤ Afterwards, discuss notable structural features of the story, such as the opening, build up, climax or series of climactic events, gradual resolution and so on. Ask the children to identify the freeze-frames/ tableaux that reflected these features. More simply, the freeze-frames representing the beginning, middle and end of the tale could be identified and grouped together.

⑥ Ask the groups to title their freeze-frames. These titles could describe the moment in the narrative or reflect one particular character's thoughts. The latter creates a perspectival summary, the former a more factual résumé.

⑦ Listen to the titles with the accompanying freeze-frames shown again so the full tale is told in summary form. If a picture book is the basis, turn the pages silently as the tale unfolds (this is ideal if you have a Big Book version). If it is a novel, just hear and see the summaries as represented in the freeze-frames.

⑧ Scribe the titles or characters' thoughts, whichever you and the children have chosen, on the board. Discuss the story's structural features again in relation to this word summary.

⑨ Invite the class to select one dramatic incident shown in a freeze-frame and subtitled on the board. They should work in pairs to produce one quality paragraph

that fleshes out the incident in detail, without straying into the next piece of action. Then retell the story by reading the paragraphs in order, with the titles of any 'missing' paragraphs read out too.

## Moving on

● Make an instant class zigzag book, or pairs could make their own with the subtitles or thoughts and accompanying illustrations.

● Share the retold tale in physical form in an assembly, with narrators, subtitles on card, or – as a recreation of the narrative – have the children voice the thoughts of the characters.

● Recreate one or two critical freeze-frames from the heart of the narrative and, as a class, voice the thoughts as an interior monologue of the main character (see page 32). Diary writing might then follow.

Page
23

**Searching the dump**

# Comic-strip capers

This activity draws attention to story structures within the medium of comics. Popular culture texts, such as comics and animation videos, can stimulate children's engagement in the learning objectives of the traditional curriculum – the comics acting as bait to capture their interests! In most cases, comic stories work like stories in any genre, having structures that can be analysed, compared, contrasted and adapted. A chronology of events can be discussed and explained using comic/cartoon frames. Try to use the kinds of comics that target the child buyer of comics rather than the parent. Be aware that more and more magazines aimed at children are in fact disguised teaching tools, rather than entertainment for children. For this activity, the intention is to encourage children's interest in curriculum learning by using literature that has direct appeal to them. These will include computer-game magazines, traditional titles such as *The Beano* and *The Dandy*, girls' magazines like *Barbie* and *Girl Talk* and other comics and sport magazines.

## Literature links

Have comics and magazines in the classroom library and let children get used to having access to a wide variety of text types and written media. Children may have spare back-copies lying around in cupboards or under their beds, so ask them to bring them in. Dennis the Menace and his sidekick Gnasher are still popular characters, along with other favourites in *The Beano* and *The Dandy*. A glance through the titles in any large newsagent will give you an idea of different genres represented in the comics world. Fantasy and science fiction are well represented, particularly because of the computer games industry; try *Sonic the Comic* for example. There are also lots of adventure comics, stories with familiar settings and, of course, humour. This type of material often provides a main source of leisure reading for children of this age. The older girls will enjoy *Girl Talk*, but boys will probably recoil from such titles, so be aware of this 'gender phobia' and try to pick a magazine with universal appeal. Look at the structures of the storylines and pick out some that are clear and have an explosive finish. Books such as the adventures of Asterix and Tintin are useful, and Marcia Williams' comic-strip retellings are worth examining, although these are longer texts and more complex in construction.

## What to do

❶ Get hold of copies of popular comics that contain complete stories. Don't forget that there are plenty of titles that may well match the text type you are currently reading and writing with the children (they can help you with this selection). Ask them before this main activity to brainstorm different titles that suit different genres. Encourage them to explain what aspects of a title make it appropriate for a certain genre.

❷ Cut up different comic strip stories into individual frames and ask pairs of children to put their allocated story together again. Leave out the final frame, so the children don't yet know the ending to the story. Encourage them to read all the frames first, then discuss and agree on an order.

❸ Once they have put the story together, ask the children to choose one frame that they feel is the most important part of the story – probably the crisis point or turning point. This exercise will lead to interesting debate and encourage the children to think hard about narrative structure.

❹ Ask the pairs to speculate on what happens at the end and make a final frame for the comic strip. Then let them look at the frame from the comic. Encourage them to note how dramatic it is and compare it with their own ideas.

❺ Provide time for the children to retell these stories orally before converting them to written stories. They could do this in small groups, perhaps as mini-performances to the whole class. Perhaps let the children decide which ending to include in the performance, if their version differs from the original.

### Moving on

● Help children to make a comic strip representation of a well-known story in shared or guided writing. You may want to use intriguing tales like 'The Tailor's Button' (page 86), 'The Rajah's Big Ears' (page 91) or 'Anansi and Postman Snake' (page 94). Make sure that the comic stories will have a destination and a purpose, perhaps put in a class book or school magazine or made into an attractive display.

● Investigate and read a variety of comic stories with the children, hunting for more examples of climactic or explosive events in the stories.

# Film frames

This activity gives children the opportunity to use film knowledge to learn about structure in traditional storytelling media. They will think about the order of events in a film and how this produces engaging effects. Children will enjoy encountering films in the classroom and applying their knowledge of them to schoolwork. Bringing film into the classroom can also help to reduce the alienation felt by children who meet stories more often on the screen than on the page.

## Literature links

Film narratives can be used to teach structure across a range of traditional text types, as films can be categorised according to narrative type. There is a wealth of films retelling traditional stories that can be used, but popular films such as the *Toy Story* films, *The Lion King*, *A Bug's Life*, *Ice Age*, *Shrek* and *Finding Nemo* tend to have similar structures that work like many stories in print form. Just as with a book, children should have the opportunity to watch the whole film through at some point.

## What to do

1 If possible, choose a film that all of the children have seen. Select a clip from an important stage of the story. It may be a crisis point or moment of great suspense.

2 Introduce the film and ask the children to name the characters and identify the setting. Avoid discussing the plot in detail at this stage. If children are not used to talking in school about films they watch in their leisure time, this should be a stimulating opportunity.

3 Show the clip and allow the children to enjoy it. Ask them to discuss in pairs what has happened before this excerpt. Then ask them to discuss what comes after it.

4 Using one character's perspective, construct an 'excitement graph' to cover the whole film. Plot important events in the story in terms of their excitement, highlighting the position of the clip you have just shown. Show time on the horizontal axis, and level of excitement on the vertical axis, and identify half a dozen highly significant events in the narrative. Write a couple of words to describe these and place them on the graph. For example, in *The Lion King*, the events might include Mufasa's death and Simba making new friends. The children need to decide if these are emotionally high or low points from the chosen character's point of view.

5 Ask the children to write a paragraph to describe one moment chosen from the excitement graph. Suggest they choose their favourite part of the film. You could model this for the clip you have shown.

## Moving on

● For further discussion on structure, cover the screen while you play another clip from the film. Can the children identify the point in the story from the soundtrack?

● Organise the children into groups of three or four to create a freeze-frame of a favourite part of the film. Advise them to create a scene with their own bodies. Ask the other children to guess what the scene is. This will show the children that they already know a great deal about how stories are put together.

# Chapter Two

# Characterisation

**Characterisation is one of the most influential ingredients of narrative since the characters co-create the story. The type of characters who inhabit a story will determine the way events unfold and the feelings that the story evokes in its readers. For example, ogres, giants and goblins will herald fear, menace and conflict, whilst stories that have warm, furry, soft characters may invoke loving and secure feelings. Character has such a determining and powerful role that children will often refer to a story predominantly by mentioning the characters in it. Indeed, character significance is shown by how common it is for story titles to carry the name of the key characters.**

The characters in a story can often act as a way to judge our own and others' moral actions and activities, by becoming the focus of exploration and debate. Critical debate about a character's thoughts, deeds and personality calls for a range of higher-order reading skills that challenge and extend the reading competence and interpretation abilities of young readers. Children should try to understand a character and his or her speech and actions by an examination of cause – both physical and emotional. To do this, children need the capacity to empathise and connect with characters' feelings and predicaments.

Seven- to nine-year-olds will be able to make connections between the characters in the stories they read with characters in their own lives, including themselves. It is important that the books selected for the classroom increase the possibility of this happening. Select well-written stories that reflect the children's cultures and backgrounds and have characters or types of characters with whom they are less familiar.

An exploration of characterisation may begin with children talking about heroes and heroines from familiar stories. The National Literacy Strategy encourages teachers to immerse children in a variety of narratives. For example, within a three-week unit on traditional tales, the children will have the opportunity to actively engage with the plight of various characters, identify and discuss main and recurring characters and evaluate their behaviour and personalities and their functions in the story. During these discussions, the children should also be justifying their views.

In order to fully understand a character, role-playing, hot-seating and involvement in a variety of drama techniques can help. You might consider, for example, what the conversations were between the witch and the caged Hansel. Children can bring a character off the page by 'becoming' that character in dramatic situations and exploring the ensuing actions and thoughts of that person.

Critical discussion of how writers create their characters will also form an important part of

the learning process. Children will be becoming aware of how authors describe the appearance, personality and behaviour of people in the stories they write. They need to have plenty of experience of reading and hearing about characters, becoming characters and discussing characters. From this foundation they can proceed to create, with you modelling the planning, drafting, editing and presenting of characters in stories. The children may, for example, write general character sketches, but with the focus on small details that can evoke sympathy or dislike, or they may focus on individual characters and retell the tale from their perspective. The activities suggested in this chapter are designed to help you and the children examine characters in more open-ended and creative ways.

© Chris Kelly

Picture books are frequently used in the character activities that follow, as they can be a sophisticated as well as an attractive medium of literature, many of which are appropriate for children in the later stages of primary school. They are a valuable resource for the Literacy Hour, both for reasons of their brevity and valuable literary content.

**Children's literature contains many colourful and memorable characters, for example Clarice and her brother Kurt in the Clarice Bean stories by Lauren Child (Orchard), Mrs Wobble the Waitress in the *Happy Families* series by Allan Ahlberg (Puffin), and animal characters like the eponymous Slow Loris by Alexis Deacon (Red Fox). Gillian Cross also draws clearly defined characters in *The Dark Behind the Curtain* (OUP) and *The Great Elephant Chase* (Puffin).**

# The name game

This activity helps children understand connections between themes and characters' names. Children will appreciate features of characterisation that can be depicted in their own stories. The activity will support them in inventing their own rich and rounded characters whose names epitomise them.

## Literature links

The children will be most inspired by stories where characters' names reflect the theme: *Mad Dog McGraw* by Myron Uhlberg (Puffin) or *The True Story of the 3 Little Pigs* by Jon Scieszka (Puffin), *Fungus the Bogeyman* by Raymond Briggs (Puffin) and *Amazing Grace* by Mary Hoffman (Frances Lincoln), the Hairy Maclary stories by Lindley Dodd (Puffin) and Pongwiffy stories by Kaye Umansky (various publishers), *Mrs Wobble the Waitress* by Janet and Allan Ahlberg (Puffin) and many of Roald Dahl's stories. *Name Games* by Theresa Breslin (Mammoth) also plays on changing names and the consequences of this.

## What to do

❶ Gather a collection of familiar books with easily recognisable characters. Use these to brainstorm the names of as many characters as the children can remember.

❷ Help the children to categorise the names into, for example, *strange, funny, nasty, scary, sweet, awe-inspiring, silly, beautiful.*

❸ Discuss how authors sometimes use names to help their readers understand some features of their characters, for example in *The Minpins* by Roald Dahl.

❹ From a collection of names in a basket or box, ask the children to take one at random and describe to a partner what this person might look like, how they might behave, what they like doing and so on. Choose very suggestive examples, such as Bilbo Baggins, Mrs Wobble the Waitress, Alfred the Great, Mrs Twit, Violet Beauregarde, Aunt Petunia, Ron Weasley, Flat Stanley. Ask children to share some of the examples with the class. Briefly extend this into a guessing game, where the children pick out a character to describe and other children work out who it is.

❺ Ask the children in pairs to construct a CV for one of their characters. Let them see a sample CV to help them with structure and wording. Encourage them to include detail in the *Interests/Hobbies* section.

## Moving on

● Ask the children to select a category from those discussed and create names to fit. Help them to use appropriate vocabulary to describe the characters.

● The children could sketch their chosen character and annotate it with personal attributes suggested by the name.

# What are they saying?

**This activity involves the children in adopting roles and improvising, creating characters and reflecting upon their behaviour, speech, attitudes, feelings and interactions with other characters. Gaps in the text, such as unrecorded conversations or those mentioned only in passing, are filled in order to gain a clearer sense of the character in action. Oral drafting in drama can lead to writing playscripts, reported speech, persuasive dialogue, letters reporting on the conversation, notes from a police interview and so on. The example described here focuses on persuasive writing and uses the role-play to generate, shape and rehearse ideas identified from a character's perspective.**

## What to do

❶ Select a tense moment from a class text to explore. Read up to this point and invite the children to create the possible problematic or persuasive conversation. Reading an earlier part of the conversation will help to set the scene.

❷ Invite the children in pairs to take up character roles and improvise the conversation at this moment in the text. This should generate a variety of ideas.

❸ After a few minutes, intervene and ask the pairs to combine into groups of four, encouraging those in similar roles to work together. The same role-play is then revisited, with two children representing one character.

## Literature links

Almost any narrative text will support this role-play, but selecting from it a challenging moment for one of the characters is essential.

Persuasion is a key feature in many texts. For example, in *Rats!* by Pat Hutchins (Red Fox), Sam tries to persuade his mum to let him have a pet rat. In *Bad Girls* by Jacqueline Wilson (Yearling), Tanya tries to persuade Mandy to accompany her shoplifting. In *Angry Arthur* by Hiawyn Oram (Red Fox), Arthur wants to stay up and watch television. In *Cliffhanger* by Jacqueline Wilson (Corgi), Dad tries to cajole a reluctant Tim into going on an adventure holiday. Stories that raise issues are particularly suitable for role-play; role-play can contribute to understanding of the characters' perspectives.

© Chris Kelly

This will involve
sharing and agreeing
ideas and generating new ones.

④ List on the board the key elements of the character's persuasive argument.

⑤ Split the class in half, with each half taking up one role. Re read the previous section of the story and improvise together the persuasive argument. Make use of the points listed on the board and draw on some of the ideas developed in the earlier role-plays.

⑥ Capture the argument in shared writing, having discussed the perspective, attitude and motivation of the characters as expressed through their words and intonation (notice typographical features and synonyms for *said* to help with this). The new piece of writing could then be compared to the author's version.

⑦ Read the new conversation together, with each half of the class voicing their allocated role and you reading any narrator's commentary if this has been included. Evaluate and improve the writing through discussion and re-reading.

⑧ To enrich the words spoken, generate speech verbs to describe the conversational manner, reflected in the reading. Adverbs could also be added.

⑨ Ask the children to continue the conversation in their original pairings. Discuss whether the characters will maintain their perspective on the conversation topic or will shift. Encourage them to explore ways of expressing this through dialogue and tone of voice.

⑩ Invite pairs of children to read their work aloud. Reflect on the characters' feelings, behaviour and relationship shown through their words, actions and tone of voice.

## Moving on

● Re-read the class composition or the paired writing. Focusing on one character, help the children to identify the key descriptors, phrases and words that provide a sense of the characters. To enrich this further, interior monologues could be undertaken (see page 32) and possibly diary entries written by one of the characters the night after the incident or argument happened. This will involve writing in the first person in role as a character in the text and will be enriched by the improvisational work.

● Re-read the story or chapter and ask the children to clap each time the author describes a character. Passages from the text could also be examined more closely for further evidence of a character's speech, action and feelings.

● Use the shared writing piece as a basis for teaching the role of narrative action in dialogue. Demonstrate, for example, how Mum leaving the room angrily or Arthur throwing a tantrum and running upstairs can temporarily or completely end the dialogue. Alternatively, the shared writing could be turned into a playscript, via genre exchange, where the dialogue is turned into another form of writing, and the narrator's voice can be compared with the stage directions.

"Don't cry Cinderboy all will be well"
"Who....what.....are you?" Stammered Cinderboy in amazement.
"I'm your fairy godmother!"
"I don't believe in fairies -that's kids stuff" Cinderboy replied
"Well try me" said the pink face. "Pick up two peanuts and put them infront of the TV."
"Why?"
"You'll do as you're told if you really want to play in the Big Cup Final!"
"Okay – Okay – there you are"
"Abracadabra" she cried and waved a long wand. There before him lay a pair of brand new football boots with rainbow laces. They fitted perfectly.
"But I've nothing to wear" moaned Cinderboy
"Abracadabra" she cried again and he was wearing the full Royal Palace kit.
"Hey, this is well cool – thanks" said Cinderboy
"But how will I get there?"
"Give me a chance!" "One thing at a time -I'm not a miracle maker you know."

# Interior monologues

In this activity, children voice the private thoughts of a story character at particularly tense or challenging moments in the narrative. Instead of some individuals suggesting how the character feels, in response to your questions, this activity encourages all the children to think out loud as the character and project themselves into the role. This can encourage empathy and a closer engagement with the character's predicament, leading to greater understanding of the character and his or her function in the narrative.

The activity can be organised through everyone simultaneously speaking the character's thoughts out loud, or a chair (or other prop) can be used to symbolise the character and children are invited to step forward, touch the chair or prop, and voice the character's inner thoughts in role. This is a useful strategy for examining a character's emotional stance, his or her perspective, feelings and motivation in a given situation. It is a valuable precursor to developing characterisation in shared writing.

## Literature links

In many narrative texts for children the main character experiences some kind of challenge or dilemma. This moment is often the most suitable for exploration in an interior monologue. For example, in *Cinderboy* by Laurence Anholt (Orchard), what might Cinderboy be thinking when he sees that the glass-studded football boot fits his stepbrother? In *The Minpins* by Roald Dahl (Puffin), Little Billy is imagining the Forest of Sin, and the Devil whispers in his ear to tempt him to visit it. The

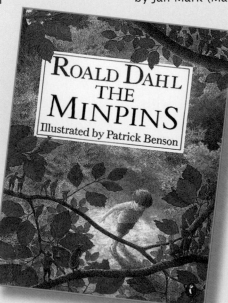

thoughts of both figures could be examined through this drama convention. In *My Frog and I* by Jan Mark (Mammoth), how does Jane feel when her little toy frog Bugsy is kidnapped? In 'Little River Turtle' (page 88), when Turtle is stranded beneath the rock in the desert, lost and alone, an interior monologue would allow his thoughts and fears to be voiced. Razvani's dilemma with the Fire-Fiend in Philip Pullman's *The Firework-Maker's Daughter* (Scholastic) could also be explored through this technique.

## What to do

➊ Select a moment from a recent or current class story in which a key character is challenged or placed in a difficult situation. For example, at the very beginning of *The Minpins*, Little Billy is bored at home; his mother keeps checking he is safe whilst he stares out of the window and dreams about the Forest of Sin just outside. His desire to visit this forbidden place is very strong, and he is *awfully tired of being good*.

➋ Read up to a suitable description in the narrative, for example when Little Billy is kneeling on his chair *gazing with longing* through the window; then break off to ponder aloud what the character might be feeling. What is the dilemma? What thoughts might be going through the character's head? What is Billy hoping? How does he feel about the Forest of Sin? Is he intrigued, tempted, but a bit frightened at the same time?

➌ Organise the children to form a circle, and place a chair in the centre of the circle. Explain that the chair can be used to represent the character (in this case, Little Billy). You could put an icon on the chair, for example two plaited ropes to represent Goldilocks' hair, or a simple toy turtle to represent Little Turtle.

➍ Re-read the scene leading up to the 'crisis' moment, then explain to the class that together you are going to try to voice the character's thoughts. Ask the children to turn to their neighbour in the circle and suggest ideas, thoughts and phrases that might be running through the character's head. Offer a few ideas yourself, for example, as Little Billy: *If I slip out quietly, perhaps Mum won't hear me go; I am*

*scared – what if there really are beasts and a Spittler in there?; Surely it's just a wood, no harm could come to me – there'll only be people walking dogs...* Preparation time is essential to help the children think forwards and gain confidence through sharing and shaping their ideas with others.

➎ When the class is prepared, model a full interior monologue by stepping forward, touching the chair and voicing the character's thoughts. Invite children to step forward and speak out loud the feelings and fears the character is experiencing. No order is necessary; some children will step forward eagerly, others may wait until impelled to do so by the train of thoughts voiced, some may not speak at all. This is all fine.

© Chris Kelly

➏ Through joint composition on the board, record some of the thoughts that Little Billy might have had that day when he was bored, wanting to explore and wanting to be 'naughty'. Through discussion, try to make the various suggestions believable and consistent with what they know about the story and characters so far. They do not, however, need to be consistent with one another: Little Billy may well have been thinking about both the pros and cons of climbing out of the window.

❼ Read on in your story. In *The Minpins*, read past the section in which Billy's mother warns him about the Forest to when the Devil/his conscience tempts Billy and tries to persuade him to come into the woods. Do not read the descriptions of the inside of the wood, but suggest the children turn to their partners and suggest what might tempt a young boy to climb out of his window and explore the Forest. For example, there may be football fields and giant playgrounds, computer games and consoles hanging from trees, television-screen shrubs, or sweets growing from the ground!

❽ This time, model a slight variation on the interior monologue. Creep in towards the chair that you are using to represent the character (Billy) and whisper loudly the words that the Devil whispered in Little Billy's ear. Encourage the children to take up a similar stance as the tempter and offer Billy the delights they have invented for the Forest of Sin.

❾ Read this section as it appears in your book. Discuss the author's choices in comparison with the children's ideas. Stress that all are valid suggestions, and explain that all writers have to make hard choices between ideas.

❿ Ask the children to write a paragraph of the incident in the story that they have just explored – for example, Little Billy daydreaming and wanting to visit the Forest and hearing the tempter invite him in. Make it clear to the children that you want them to include some sense of the character's thoughts and feelings, which were scribed on the board.

> I wish I'd listened to mummy, my skin is dry and crispy and I'm hot, too hot. I've lost the butterfly. Where can she be? I don't know how to get back home to the river, which way should I go? My lips are cracking, I've never felt so alone.

> Go on. You're a big brave boy. Remember when you went to the shops on your own on your bike. You did that on your own. Also when mum took you to Chessington you went really high on that rollercoaster. Be brave, nothing will happen to you.

> Billy do not take your mum's foot steps. She is a scaredy cat. Are you a scaredy cat? If you do not come into the woods you will have no candy or toys. You will love the woods, there no time to waste come on! Are you a baby? She's just scared, come follow me.

## Moving on

● Let the children write individual diary entries recording as a stream of consciousness Billy's desires and thoughts that day.

● Combine two drama conventions, such as interior monologue and freeze-frame or hot-seating. Little Billy, for example, could be hot-seated by his cousins who come to stay and want to hear all about the Forest of Sin and why Billy has never been there. Used together, they can further enrich the children's writing. Reflecting upon both the conventions, discuss with the children which drama convention they felt revealed the most about the character.

● Contrast the perspective of two differently positioned characters. For example, also examining Billy's mother's thoughts during the same moment, or when she goes into the sitting room and finds him absent. In a novel, using interior monologue to generate character's reflections at significant points in the story can help the reader keep track of the character's changing emotional perspective.

# Emotion graph

**This activity explores a character's feelings and emotional stance within a narrative. It is an excellent deductive shared reading activity, and seeks to understand the character and his or her relationship to the story structure.**

## Literature links

This activity works best with books in which a core character clearly responds to challenges and adventures that befall him or her. *Willy the Wimp* by Anthony Browne (Walker Books) and *Mufaro's Beautiful Daughters* by John Steptoe (Puffin) are good examples of texts that suit emotion-mapping exercises. Novels such as Anne Fine's *The Diary of a Killer Cat* (Puffin) and *The Dinosaur's Packed Lunch* by Jacqueline Wilson (Corgi) are feasible to use, although it is more demanding to track a character's emotions through a whole novel. Strong single chapters from longer stories are also possible to use for emotion maps, providing the chapter reflects the character's changing perspective and situation.

## What to do

❶ Select a book the children already know. Discuss the images on the cover and emotive ones from inside if appropriate.

❷ Focus on the main character and discuss how this person feels at a particular moment. Ask the children to adopt positions and/or expressions that reveal the emotional stance of the character.

❸ Together read the text to notice the character's position through the story. This will begin generating the emotion map.

❹ Re-read the text. Each time the character encounters a new experience, meets someone or makes a decision, draw a simple image of his or her face and agree with the children on how s/he feels at the moment concerned. Re-read key points to draw out subtle, implicit presentations of feelings. Label the image with a key word or short phrase to describe this emotion.

❺ Continue in this way, creating a map of the character's changing emotions. The map can take any form you choose, such as cyclical, random or a shape particularly appropriate to the story.

❻ Discuss how the finished emotion map tracks the character's feelings, views and personal journey through the text. Link this to the action of the story.

❼ As a class, use the emotion map to retell the story from the character's perspective.

## Moving on

● Give story books to groups of three or four children and ask them to make emotion maps following the main characters. After oral retellings of part or all of the story, written tellings could emerge. One or two powerful paragraphs may be better than the whole narrative.

● Select a powerful or tense moment for the character, and read the events surrounding it. Use interior monologue (see page 32) to explore this. Invite volunteers to voice the character's thoughts. Let the children voice their ideas as they feel the need, and be sure to voice yours.

# My life story

In this activity, children take part in role-play around characters in a class reading book. Character improvisation and role-play demands children's close attention to the characters they are playing and encourages them to think about the traits of character they possess. This will enable the children to draw on these experiences when they attempt their own writing and explore characters of their own making in a story narrative. The activity is based on the television series *This is Your Life* and uses the main character of the story (or at least a particularly interesting character) as the central figure of the show. A child takes on this role while others take the parts of other characters in the story (or other characters mentioned or implied who do not make an appearance). You should take on the role of compère. If the children are not familiar with the programme and you have an ERA licence, tape an edition and play excerpts from it either at the end of a day or as a form of shared reading in the Literacy Hour.

## What to do

❶ Remind the children about the television programme *This is Your Life* and/or show them some excerpts. Tell them you will be asking them to perform the show in the classroom based around the characters in the story book you have chosen. Explain that you will be the compère.

❷ Decide together which character will be the focus of the show. *Whose life do we know most about or has the most interest?* Then list the other characters that will be brought on to talk about the main character. Decide in what order these figures will appear.

## Literature links

This activity can use any quality piece of literature that has a cast of interesting characters. Traditional stories work well, as do many modern picture books. Lauren Child's series of books about Clarice Bean (Orchard) makes use of a lovely collection of characters that children would enjoy role-playing. Equally, one of the animals from *The Wind in the Willows* by Kenneth Grahame, or Badger from *Badger's Parting Gifts* by Susan Varley (Picture Lions) would work well.

A programme with a similar format to *This is Your Life* could easily be based on the Rajah in the tale of 'The Rajah's Big Ears' (see page 91). Children's novels such as *Too Big!* by Geraldine McCaughrean (Corgi) or Berlie Doherty's *Street Child* (Lions) also contain rich characters who can be welcomed onto the *This is Your Life* podium. The relations between characters are emphasised when the children are asked to describe their association with the key personality on the show.

❸ Divide the class into 'character groups' of four or five children who need to decide amongst themselves what their character will say about the focus character. They should also decide, by themselves if possible, which of them will perform the role-play. Make sure everyone understands that even if they are not role-playing, they have a very important job imagining and deciding on the kind of things the character will say. For example, you might have a Marcie group from *Clarice Bean, That's Me* by Lauren Child, or a barber group from 'The Rajah's Big Ears'. One child from each group will need to volunteer to take up the character's role in the television show.

❹ Loosely arrange the classroom to accommodate 'on-stage' seating for the main character and the guests. Plan beforehand where the participants and audience are to go and ask children before the lesson begins to be the stagehands (furniture movers).

❺ Start the show by introducing the character who is the subject of the programme, filling in any gaps you don't know about his or her life where necessary. You can briefly 'interview' the character to help with this if the child is confident in the role. Introduce each guest and allow him or her to talk in role about the main guest and their relationship. They can make up anecdotes about them or, more simply, recall events that have occurred in the story. This is the challenging but creative part and really encourages children to get inside the story you have been reading.

❻ As the host, close the show by thanking the guests and presenting the red book to the main character.

## Moving on

● After the show is over, generate a more relaxed, informal atmosphere and discuss the relationships between the characters and why each guest said what they did about the subject character.

● Before each guest is introduced in the real show, the voice of the guest makes a short comment about the subject figure. The audience is encouraged to guess who s/he is from the comments. The children could write and read these comments for mystery introductions.

# Characters' rooms

The purpose of this activity is to help children develop a full sense of the characters they include in their stories and to learn more than one way in which characterisation can be shown and developed. In a playful way at first, the illustration and annotations created can be used to construct a character's domestic background to add depth and colour to the children's character portrayals. Children at this age will understand the relationship between their own interests and hobbies and what is contained in their bedroom, for example, and will be able to make a connection like this for story characters. This will help them develop a personal and effective response to characters in existing stories and will also help them to create character pen-portraits of their own.

## What to do

❶ Start by reading *The True Story of the 3 Little Pigs*, or your chosen text, emphasising the ironic personal narrative. (Once the children have understood that they can make decisions about the 'true' nature of the character, other similar stories could be introduced and discussed.) Present the possibility that the character of the wolf may have been misjudged, as he is suggesting, and ask the children to consider the possible true nature of the wolf. They will probably (as they should if they are able to grasp the ironies in Alexander T Wolf's version) still see him as the Big Bad Wolf.

❷ Talk about where clues about the wolf's personality may exist, for example in his house – perhaps on his bookshelves; his

## Literature links

This activity will be most appropriate with a character from a known story where more than one interpretation of events and characters can be made, for example with alternative, subverted versions of traditional tales. A perfect choice would be *The True Story of the 3 Little Pigs* by Jon Scieszka (Puffin), where the use of irony and point of view offers the children a glimpse of a subtextual meaning. A more straightforward example, but for children who can manage a more print-focused text, *Mr Cool* by Jacqueline Wilson (Kingfisher) gives the

capacity to develop all four main characters through these activities. Jeremy Strong's books, and in particular *The Karate Princess* (Puffin), also offer opportunities for children to be playful around characterisation in this way.

choice of decoration and posters, ornaments, photographs; in his larder and so on. Make connections with the children's own personalities and hobbies and the objects they might find in the homes that indicate they are friendly, for example displays of photographs of friends, letters and gifts from friends and relations.

❸ If you are using *The True Story of the 3 Little Pigs* for this activity, ask the children to design a bedroom or another room for Alexander T Wolf, providing clues that a reader could use to determine his innocence or guilt in killing the little pigs and the honesty/accuracy of his portrayal of himself. For example, in his kitchen would he have vegetarian cookbooks on his bookshelf and a photograph of his granny, or would there be recipe cards on how to cook pig, half-eaten bones, rabbits' ears and other leftovers on grubby plates? What might books on his bedside table be called?

❹ Ask the children to add brief annotations to support and explain their room design and help a reader notice the details they have included. It might be helpful for the children to work in pairs for this part of the activity, as the devil is in the detail and their imaginative justification of it.

❺ Provide an opportunity for the children to use the details of their drawings as evidence in the wolf's court case. Create a whole class improvisation of the court scene, with you and the children in role as Alexander T, the Third Little Pig, the cops, lawyers for defence and prosecution, judge, jury and so on.

## Moving on

● Invite the children to extend the original story with their own additions, answering questions about the wolf's home life by having, for example, the wolf write a prison diary or create a new recipe for a cookbook or write a letter about his eventful day to his Uncle Terrible Big Bad Wolf.

● The children could also do this activity for a central character in their own stories they are drafting. They could be challenged to make use of some of these character clues in their writing.

● Introduce the children to other 'Big Bad Wolf' books that offer alternative, non-traditional perspectives, such as *Little Wolf's Diary of Daring Deeds* by Ian Whybrow (HarperCollins), *Mr Wolf's Pancakes* by Jan Fearnley (Mammoth) and *Wolf Academy* by Jonathan Allen (Orchard). Would these wolves have different kitchens or bedrooms?

# Horoscopes

This activity encourages children to think hard about characters in stories they have been reading by exploration through the popular practice of horoscopes. As with any story that contains magic or other mystical matters, you will need to be sensitive about the beliefs and values of children in your class. The activity can help children provide further detail about characters in their own story compositions. It asks them to use their knowledge of stories they have heard or read to write a horoscope for a character that appeals to them. The link between reading and writing is a key to becoming a good author and children in this activity brush with the world of Mystic Meg and Russell Grant to introduce an alternative model for writing about characters. You will need to hunt around in family newspapers and magazines to search out good examples of horoscopes that are not too detailed. This is a bit of fun with learning embedded in it, as the children will enjoy looking up their own star sign and assessing how close their own life is to the predictions. Have some fun identifying the different star signs and the characteristics of those who fall under these signs. Do the children know their own star signs? Does the description fit them?

## Literature links

Any of the characters found in the children's/class's current or recent reading books should fit this activity. Some suggestions that would work well, however, are: Harry Potter, Dudley or Uncle Vernon from JK Rowling's Harry Potter stories (Bloomsbury), Andy from *The Suitcase Kid* by Jacqueline Wilson (Yearling) or Plop from *The Owl Who Was Afraid of the Dark* by Jill Tomlinson (Mammoth). Equally, you could use characters found in short picture books, as well as those found in traditional stories – the wolf in 'Little Red Riding Hood', for instance, or Little Turtle himself (see page 88). In children's magazines and television guides, astrologers often describe the characters of those who have certain star signs, so these magazines would be useful to have available too.

do not pick flowers

Horoscope for Little red riding Hood

The stars tell me that you should stay on the path dont stop and pick flowers for you will meet a wicked stranger, but fear not for a fairy with a sting will save you and you will never see the likes of that particular stranger again!

by Jessica

## What to do

❶ Show the children lots of examples of horoscope writing found in light family or children's magazines. Ask them to pick out any notable features. For example, many horoscopes describe the planets' movements at the moment and how this affects what happens to people under certain star signs.

❷ Using a story character from current reading, discuss what star sign s/he may be. Encourage the children to tell you why they think as they do, referring to feelings, events, decisions and so on that have occurred so far in the story.

❸ As a shared activity with you as scribe, write a horoscope for a chosen character that hints at what may happen to him or her in the story. This should provoke rich discussion. Use the horoscopes that you have looked at as a class as a guide. For example, a horoscope for Plop the Barn Owl on the day he goes to visit the old lady (in the chapter 'Dark is kind' in *The Owl Who Was Afraid of the Dark*) might involve: a) deciding on his star sign, b) agreeing to hint at what is about to come, and c) describing his expected feelings at this point.

❹ Remember that shared writing works well when the teacher 'thinks aloud' about the writing s/he is doing. Make sure the children are given the chance to contribute to the decisions made about the writing, and weave in their words and phrases and their general ideas. When the horoscope is drafted, read it back as a class, looking together for ways to improve it. This models what real writers need to do. Once the text has been read through for composition, you may wish to proofread it for transcription errors or ways to improve it at word and sentence level. For most children, it is difficult to concentrate on composition and transcription at the same time, so work on these stages of writing separately.

❺ Ask the children to work in pairs to write a horoscope for another character from the same story. Specify a particular moment in the narrative to focus on.

## Moving on

● In the style of magazines, decide what star sign a character from a story is and make a 'love it or hate it' list of activities this character would or would not want to be involved with. You could call it the 'Blissful and Stressful' list of things. Decide whether this should be a whole-class or paired activity based upon the children's experience of astrology. For example, Little Red Riding Hood could be an Aquarius, so her 'Blissful' list might include shopping with her mother in the market. Her 'Stressful' list might include talking to strange creatures in the woods!

# Silhouette and quote

In this activity, children consider what characters reveal about themselves through what they say and how they interact, particularly in dialogue, with other characters. As they become more familiar with the characters they meet in different stories, they can begin to predict their actions, feelings about, and responses to events that occur in the story. This activity encourages children to imagine what characters might say beyond the text frame, when they are placed in different situations. Good characterisation in stories can be seen in part in the way writers acquaint their readers with their characters, making readers engage and empathise with them. Practice of this kind of high-level reading skill will help children develop their insights about character construction. The activity also involves some art and design work, asking children to make silhouettes. This hybrid of an activity gets them active and creatively involved with story characters. The activity works best if used as an ongoing activity that the children continue in their 'own' time. You will need to introduce it and promote it in literacy time, but the children can write their quotes at spare moments in the day, or as they are inspired! Alternatively, you may wish to make a more formal session out of it.

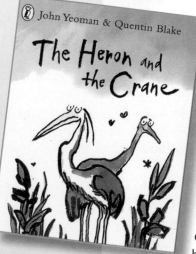

## Literature links

Draw on the characters that appear in the genre of fiction you are reading in a unit of work, or encourage children to think about characters from the class novel. Characters in the following books have been used with success: *The Heron and the Crane* by John Yeoman (Puffin), *Zoo* by Anthony Browne (Red Fox), *Willa and Old Miss Annie* by Berlie Doherty (Walker), *Pure Dead Wicked* by Debi Gliori (Corgi), or *The BFG* by Roald Dahl (Puffin).

John Yeoman & Quentin Blake

The Heron and the Crane

## What to do

1 Ask the children to help you choose a favourite character or one from current reading to focus on. Start off by reading focal points of the story, then help the children to draw simple silhouettes. Shining the light of an overhead projector onto a wall with paper attached to it will help you to draw good silhouettes: the shape of the face is drawn round and then cut out and transferred to black sugar paper where it is cut out again. A hat, distinctive hairstyle, spectacles or other details can be added at this stage to fit the character. If you don't want to do it this

way, many children are happy to copy outlines of illustrations from books onto black paper and cut them out.

❷ When the children have finished making their silhouettes, pin their drawings onto a board low enough to give children easy access to them. This could form part of a display in the reading area.

❸ Next, provide some blank speech bubbles (to attach with Blu-Tack) for children to write in and place alongside a particular character's silhouette. Encourage the children to think of phrases or questions that typify this character's attitudes or behaviour. If the children are working in pairs, they could develop possible suggestions with their response partners, but they will need to focus on a particular moment in the story to generate ideas, or they could focus on the theme. For example, the theme of *The Heron and the Crane* is one of love and different views, so the heron may say, '*I wouldn't marry you if you provided all the fish in this pond.*'

❹ The activity can be a single lesson or an ongoing activity that you introduce in a lesson. You can encourage the children to work on the writing in their own time, or ask each child to complete one speech bubble as part of a class activity. Alternatively, if organised as a one-lesson activity, small groups could create quotes from the character for particular moments in the text.

❺ The silhouettes and quotes created by the children could now form the basis of a valuable discussion about the language used by certain characters. Particular speech verbs and adverbs could be ascribed to certain characters.

*I wouldn't marry you if you provided all the fish in this pond.*

## Moving on

● Add thought bubbles for the children to fill in too. Discuss the difference in the nature of thoughts and speech in terms of privacy and of characters not revealing their feelings to other characters, and how this could be reflected in writing. Interior monologues could also be created to develop character thinking (also see page 32).

● The quotes could be used as the basis of some report writing about the character. For example, in a magazine interview, the quotes themselves could be employed as reported speech.

● During their reading of other stories, encourage the children to use whiteboards to note down the words and phrases of particular characters, or combine this awareness with some role-play exploration.

# Comic-strip profiles

The aim of this activity is to encourage children to explore characterisation by using the often more extreme individuals found in comics. Children will be familiar with them and will engage enthusiastically when popular culture is employed in the context of the classroom. This exploration can lead to the children drawing and devising characters for their own stories. The activity can work particularly well when exploring biography and autobiography since comic characters (such as Desperate Dan and Beryl the Peril) are very memorable, have marked characteristics and personalities and recognisable backgrounds/social circles/environments. Some comics are now more sophisticated, employing links to television shows, computer games and other media texts. Don't be put off! Keep up with developments in children's media, and remember to ask the children about what they are reading at the moment or what pastimes they are particularly enjoying. In other words, keep your finger on the pulse of children's popular culture and look for comics, magazines and books that reflect their current interests.

## Literature links

Collect examples of all the old favourites as well as the newer, computer-game or movie tie-in types of comics. Children will normally have plenty at home too that they might be willing to bring in. Try *Sonic the Comic*, *The Dandy*, *The Beano*, *Nickleodeon*, *Looney Tunes* and perhaps *Goosebumps*, for example. You will find many comics and magazines that are rather gender-specific; these still have their uses, but remember to differentiate. Sadly, boys sometimes respond very negatively to texts aimed at girls. Lively and vividly realised characters from well-known fiction could also be used for an adapted version of this activity.

Dennis is always doing naughty tricks. He is very clever and he has good plans, but Dennis is selfish and seems to enjoy playing tricks on other people. Just for fun he tricks policemen, his mum and dad and thinks it is a laugh. His dog is called Gnasher because he likes biting the postman and anyone else. Dennis really is a menace! But he is a fun one.

## What to do

❶ Bring in a range of comic-strip stories and ask the children to help you too with this. They may have hundreds stacked away at home somewhere and may be willing to bring some in. You will have to look through the ones they contribute, in case some are inappropriate for the age range in your class.

❷ If possible (and if the comics are not particularly precious to their owners), get the children to cut out some of their favourite characters from the comics. For this activity, the bigger the picture, the better! Ask the children to paste each one onto a separate sheet of A3 paper, so that each child has a picture of their chosen character.

❸ As a class introduction, select one of the characters the children have chosen and who is well known to all of them, and show them how to brainstorm everything they know about that figure: how old s/he is, where she lives, what her temper is like, what kind of tricks she gets involved in, favourite foods, parents, clothes, pastimes, history, friends and so on. You could make up some specific questions

about the character for the children to supply real or imagined answers. For example: *What significant event occurred to this character when she was young? What are her favourite sweets? Who in the world would she really like/hate to meet or spend time with? What is this character's favourite article of clothing and why? Who is her best friend? What sort of thing do they get up to together?*

❹ Ask the children to write their ideas along these lines around the cut-out picture of their character. Explain that these sheets will later be displayed as posters in the classroom. The children will enjoy talking about their chosen character and sharing their knowledge of that character's particular traits in pairs. The picture will help to remind them, and you will be surprised at how much the children know and can recall.

❺ In a plenary, instead of asking each pair of children to read out their character profiles, why not ask them to display their work around the classroom (temporarily attached with Blu-Tack) and let all of the children walk around, reading the comments. Then share some notable observations from the sheets. Were some of the children surprised at other children's interpretations of the same character? Which character sounds fun or nasty to know? Which would make a good friend? Why?

⑥ Discuss elements of the character profiles that are 'fact' – information that the text explicitly tells us about the character – and those that are wholly invented by the children or otherwise at least partly based on the children's inference and deduction from the text.

## Moving on

● Ask the children to give a short oral biography of their character, using their character profile to help them. Oral rehearsal like this will require the children to begin constructing descriptive paragraphs and think about sequential order, which will support later writing.

● Ask the children to write a biographical profile similar to those found in contemporary children's magazines for pop stars and sports figures. These should use a mixture of media: the children's drawn pictures and perhaps small clipart icons as well as writing. You may want to construct a writing frame with subheadings to scaffold the children's writing.

● Consider asking the children to invent and draw a fictional cartoon/comic character of their own and repeating the activity for this figure. This profile could then be used as a basis for a story that involves this character. This could lead to rich character writing as children will have been given the opportunity to think and talk about the character over a period of time.

● This activity could also be adapted to use emotive characters from picture fiction or even unillustrated novels. Jacqueline Wilson's characters, for example, could be drawn in comic style and brainstorms created about Tracy Beaker, Biscuits from *Buried Alive!* or Tanya from *Bad Girls*.

# Chapter Three

# Story Settings

**Children experience a very visual world and quickly learn to make sense of a myriad of images around them – from television, advertisements, comics, films and computers. This early learning at home and in other contexts outside school, combined with their alertness to detail in images of all kinds, creates a useful framework for children's encounters with fiction, and in particular picture fiction during their literacy work in school.**

As children are introduced to the significance of the setting in story (as a geographical place, a social context, the characters' society, a contributor to atmosphere and mood), so are they able to make connections, however tenuous, between their own worlds and that of the narrative. Indeed, the range of picture fiction now available offers huge opportunities for children who are quick to

47

read images, and these sophisticated texts create spaces for children to inhabit the story and interpret the narrative, as they do in their own choice of texts out of school.

The place in which stories are set influences the narrative as it unfolds and also shapes the nature of the characters and their actions within the story. For example, children traditionally expect to see fairies in woodlands, bears in caves, princesses in palaces, and mermaids under the sea. If, however, the 'natural' setting is distorted, subverted or simply changed in a more subtle way, the nature of the characters and the events in the story will be influenced with interesting results. In Fiona French's book *Snow White in New York* (OUP), as soon as the author puts Snow White in a different environment her occupation, her companions, her death and the resolution of the story are all influenced by the sense of place; in this case, life in the big city. Snow White's behaviour as a city girl is markedly different from her innocence and naivety in more traditional versions and instantly places this tale within the reach and appeal of a different audience and age group of children.

The setting of a story creates a window through which the characters and events are viewed. Children need opportunities to hear, discuss, read and imagine stories with both predictable and unpredictable settings. This will encourage them to develop their own skills of description and narration in activities designed around illustrated texts. Children can use the illustrations to describe potential action or to present their own interpretation and elaboration of the story.

As children learn to investigate and understand the settings in which familiar stories are told and retold they will begin to realise how this sense of place, and the detail contained in it, can create a response in the reader or the audience.

Exploring how authors and illustrators create imagined worlds and evocative settings will support children as they attempt to set their

© Sally King

own narratives in time and place. Providing opportunities for children to depict settings and collect words and phrases to describe scenes will enhance their development as writers and authors. Enlivening tales by re-setting them in unfamiliar places, or by adding suggestive detail, will provide young writers with useful experience to build on when creating their own narratives.

Slightly more extended texts, such as *Farm Boy* by Michael Morpurgo (HarperCollins), can help children as they become more experienced readers to develop a sense of time and place in their own descriptive narratives, both oral and written. Reading and discussing the descriptive language that Morpurgo uses to create his worlds, for example, and investigating the rich vocabulary and authorial devices he uses that indicate changes in time, support young writers in using such techniques themselves. Stories set in particular periods of history, like *Farm Boy*, *A Game of Catch* by Helen Cresswell (Red Fox) or *A Parcel of Patterns* by Jill Paton Walsh (Puffin) also offer insights into different settings.

The nature and quality of the texts provided for children when focusing on this story element is very important. The work of Anthony Browne, for example *The Tunnel* (Walker Books), is renowned for the often surreal, but carefully detailed and highly emotive illustrations, which encourage young readers to forage closely for detail. More subtly perhaps, Jeannie Baker's wordless picture book, *Window* (Walker Books), evokes great emotion as the illustrative setting takes the reader and the characters on a journey through time and change. Maurice Sendak in *Where the Wild Things Are* (Red Fox) takes his readers from the familiar bedroom setting on a journey to a wild and exotic land but returns them safely home to the warm territory of supper and bedtime, offering both simple connections and an opportunity to taste the fantastic in one short book.

As children begin to manage more extended texts in print, the settings are often realistically depicted for them textually by authors such as Jacqueline Wilson in, for example, *Sleep-overs* (Corgi) or Dick King-Smith in *The Sheep-Pig* and the *Hodgeheg* (both Puffin). In *Bill's New Frock* by Anne Fine (Egmont), it is possible to create images of the school, the classroom and the playground from the view given by Bill.

Through discussion and activities, including writing, the children can begin to see that settings are often influenced and changed according to the characterisation created by the author. In this way, children will begin to understand the connections in stories between setting, character and structure.

The construction of settings, whether drawn or written, offers young readers and writers the opportunity to connect, co-create or simply visualise in their mind's eye the places in which characters dwell, encounter problems and resolve issues.

In the National Literacy Strategy, settings are given emphasis in both key stages to help teachers focus on this aspect in their planning and teaching. However, there is no clear hierarchy or particular 'right time' for introducing settings. Indeed, very young children have already been introduced to the imaginary worlds of story settings through the nursery rhymes and traditional tales recounted to them before they can read for themselves.

Children need to be offered a range and variety of settings, from stories with familiar and comforting settings to stories set in dream worlds or those representing less familiar cultures.

**It is important for children to be able to make connections between stories they encounter and their own lives, comparing, for example, Bill's school context to their own in *Bill's New Frock*. Settings can also challenge perceptions, invite questions and create uncertainty, as in David Almond's *Skellig* (Hodder). The best fiction will serve these many functions and inspire young writers to take up similar challenges.**

© Derek Cooknell

# Personal connections

The aim of this activity is to help children understand the significance of setting in the structure of a story. It will also help them to make decisions about settings as they work to construct their own texts. Leaning particularly on known and familiar places in which to establish fictional events will strengthen the children's creative potential. It is particularly important in this activity that some of the children's ideas are shaped and developed further to help them become clear about connections between character and setting and how to make these connections in their own story writing.

## Literature links

Alternative versions of traditional stories, such as *Three Cool Kids* by Rebecca Emberley (Little Brown & Co) and *Lazy Jack* or *The Three Little Pigs* by Tony Ross (both Andersen Press), would support the children in subverting the settings of familiar tales. Using traditional tales may make this activity more straightforward initially, as the children would not have to struggle to remember the detail of the text. Other texts with clear and familiar settings, such as *Voices in the Park* by Anthony Browne (Picture Corgi), would also lend themselves to this activity. This book, in fact, would be particularly useful with this age group, as it requires some sophisticated interpretations.

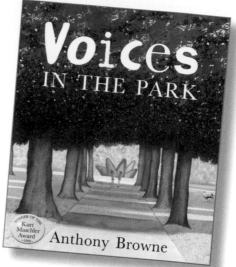

## What to do

❶ Discuss with the children the importance of setting, in general terms, drawing on two or three books as examples, identifying where they are set and why. Look, for example, at woods and forests and the connections with magic and fantasy and some of the symbolism that such settings contain.

❷ Brainstorm a wide range of potential settings for stories, linking these closely to the children's own experiences of holidays, trips, local leisure centres, parks, school and so on. Encourage the children to make these very specific so that they can be easily visualised and will serve as a reminder during their choices of other stories containing such settings

❸ Read *Voices in the Park* by Anthony Browne, or your chosen text. Make sure the children can see the illustrations. Notice how the setting changes subtly with each character's perspective.

④ Ask the children to revisit the text in pairs to identify the details of how the setting changes – what is included or excluded for each voice and why.

⑤ Still in pairs, ask the children to consider another fictional character from a different text. Encourage them to choose a less obvious character, perhaps from comics or television (Bart Simpson, for example) and look at how Anthony Browne's setting would change to accommodate this character. If Bart entered the park, he may hang out with his mates – perhaps skateboarding – and the setting may be transformed to create a more Springfield-like environment, with graffiti, scratches on the tree trunks, litter and cigarette butts around and so on.

⑥ Discuss this as a class. Using an acetate sheet over the book, include the children's examples from their paired discussion of changes to the existing key features in the setting (the bench, trees, and so on).

⑦ Invite the pairs to re-title *Voices in the Park* with the name of a new setting, for example *Voices in my Street*, *Voices in the Subway*, *Voices at the Bus Stop*, *Voices at School*, *Voices at the Scout Hut*.

⑧ Discuss how this would change the main content of the story, if at all, and how the text could nonetheless retain significant themes or characters.

⑨ In pairs, ask the children to write a section of the story in their new setting, for example *Voices at the Bus Stop*, with pairs of children contributing one of the voices. Remind the children that the emphasis is on the creation of the setting and the impact of the character on that, rather than character development.

© Derek Cooknell

## Moving on

● Provide an opportunity for groups to create story maps for a familiar story, such as 'The Three Little Pigs' or 'The Three Billy Goats Gruff', in a different but known place. The children could, for example, move these tales from the country to the town or use their own settings generated before. They should annotate their maps with specific vocabulary to focus attention on the new setting. This may involve naming objects and creating evocative noun phrases, for example *fresh green grass; lush sweet fronds; miles of fodder, juicy and crisp*. Share the completed maps or present them in a display.

● Ask the children to contribute to a bank of settings, using small sample illustrations with descriptive vocabulary attached. This ongoing collection could

be saved in a wall pocket or a 'basket of ideas' to which children could continue to contribute and from which they could draw inspiration. You might further develop this activity by encouraging them to identify a familiar setting but add an unfamiliar tone to it – such as a sinister bedroom or a safe and cosy forest. This could be organised by creating two banks of cards with the children (one for place and one for description), then they select one from each. The children could then be asked to begin an oral story-telling based on the settings generated.

# Literature Venns

This activity encourages children to focus on the importance of setting in the development of story writing by asking them to explore the difference setting makes. They use the simple form of Venn diagrams to compare different versions of one story that have clear differences in the setting. By doing so, they will notice how the setting will affect other features of the story, including characterisation, events and language use. Another advantage of this activity is that it offers children time to talk about books together. They have the opportunity to listen to each other's views and have their own views valued too. Learning can be at its richest when children are involved in animated talk. The talk here can either be teacher-guided or child-directed. The activity will also encourage children's creativity in adapting traditional stories and their structures to new contexts. Venn diagrams provide a good structure for this activity, as, when children see

information about stories portrayed graphically in this way, it helps in understanding and recall. Venns can be used to compare poems or stories by the same author too. In reading, for example, two poems by Brian Patten, children can use the structure of the Venn diagram to brainstorm the differences and similarities in structure, theme and language.

## What to do

❶ Read *Snow White in New York* to the children (or another updated traditional tale with a distinctive setting). While you are reading the story, ask the children to notice and record on whiteboards the differences between this version and others they know.

❷ Afterwards, briefly ask the children to comment on what they have noticed: they would have seen the difference in setting, the language the characters use, the way

## Literature links

This activity works particularly well with well-known narratives, such as 'original' and modernised versions of traditional stories or fairy tales. It is important that there are contrasts in the settings. *Snow White in New York* by Fiona French (OUP) is a good model, also *The Three Little Wolves and the Big Bad Pig* by Eugene Trivizas (Egmont), *Cinderboy*

by Laurence Anholt (Orchard). For older children, try Gillian Cross's *Wolf* (Puffin). This is a gritty, street-wise novel that has the Little Red Riding Hood story threaded through it. Children will relish the way all these authors manage to subvert the traditional versions of well-known stories and they will enjoy recognising the traditional features left in.

the story is told and how the events have been altered. This information can now be represented in the form of a literature Venn.

3 If the children are inexperienced in generating this kind of discussion it would be wise to start it off as a shared activity. Draw a Venn diagram on the board to pick out the similarities and differences between traditional versions and this one. Alternatively, you may wish to ask the children to compile their literature Venns in pairs. In this case, hand out photocopied Venn diagrams. Ask the children to share their suggestions noted during the reading, and show them where these fit into the Venn diagram. Features that are unique to either the traditional version or the new one are listed in the left and right sectors. Similarities are given where the circles overlap in the centre. (See the example shown, *right*.)

**Snow White in New York**

Setting: modern New York;
Jazzmen 7;
Bad female character, Queen of Underworld, likes to see herself in newspaper called 'Mirror';
Americanisms;
Prince is name of reporter;
poisoned cocktail

Plot: vain, evil stepmother tries to kill Snow White; 7 friends help Snow White; she falls in love with prince; happy ending

**Traditional Snow White**

Setting: rural – woods, castles, a long time ago;
7 dwarves;
stepmother is real queen;
fairy tale language;
real prince;
poisoned food

## Moving on

● For their own writing, ask the children to work in pairs to subvert the setting of another familiar story. Ask them to use another literature Venn to plan the differences in a similar way as their earlier Venn showed the differences between versions of 'Snow White'. Ask them to choose a well-known story, listing the key features of that story in one circle of the diagram and putting their ideas for changes in the other. Similarities can then be discussed, as before, and placed in the central section. The children can then go on to use their diagrams to assist them when they are writing their own versions of the traditional tale.

● The children's stories could be made into individual books for the classroom library. To enrich the production of their books, the children might like to use illustrations or photographs from magazines to help create the setting.

# Geographical maps

This activity encourages children to vividly imagine the geographical settings in stories. It can be linked with early map work in geography, and also encourages children to 'enter' the world of the book. By doing so, children are able to really see the world created in books, which helps them to develop their own imaginary worlds for their own stories. Accomplished readers and writers create pictures in their minds of the worlds that stories evoke. This activity makes explicit the kind of active imaginative 'tasks' involved in reading and writing. This is an important skill throughout primary school. The activity draws the emphasis of reading away from the decoding of print and places it on the meaning of the book. It is especially helpful for children who have become stuck on the technicalities of phonic de-coding and need to be reminded about why we all read in the first place!

## Literature links

Many stories, whether picture books or novels, give a strong sense of place. Often characters in the story will move around their setting on journeys or simply in their day-to-day interaction with their community. AA Milne's *Winnie-the-Pooh* and *The House at Pooh Corner* provide a map to accompany the stories that shows the Hundred Acre Wood and other characters' houses in relation to Christopher Robin and Pooh Bear. Mairi Hedderwick's Katie Morag books (Red Fox) include a picture map in the endpapers and a detailed island map in, for example, *The Big Katie Morag Storybook*. This activity can help children 'get into' more classic children's texts by asking them to create drawings, paintings or collages of the settings where the action takes place. Classic texts can prove more difficult for children to relate to than more modern ones, so this kind of activity will help. Try using it with *Tom's Midnight Garden* by Philippa Pearce (Puffin), asking the children to depict the layout of the garden in relation to the house; or 'The Rajah's Big Ears' (page 91) or 'Anansi and Postman Snake' (page 94). Modern stories can work equally well, for example *Six Dinner Sid* by Inga Moore (Hodder Wayland) or the Clarice Bean stories by Lauren Child (Orchard). Clarice has neighbours who appear in the stories (such as Robert Grainger), she goes to school, and in *What Planet Are You From, Clarice Bean?* her street becomes the focal point of much of the action.

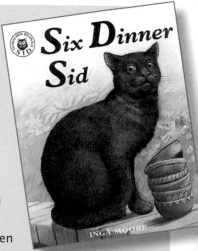

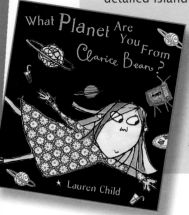

## What to do

❶ Remind the children of the characters and storyline of the book you have chosen. If possible, read the whole text again.

❷ Ask the children to speculate about the homes the characters live in and the kinds of geographical features one might encounter in the environment of the story.

❸ Ask the children to imagine a map of where the action takes place. At this point, you may wish to show an example of a map of a story setting (such as *Winnie-the-Pooh*, *The Hobbit* or Kevin Crossley-Holland's Arthur trilogy). Taking the children's suggestions, construct the map on the board. Make use of simple map-making skills the children may be developing in geography. Remind them that the pictures/icons should be small enough that all the details of the setting can be included.

❹ Give pairs of children large sheets of paper (at least A3) and ask them to draw a map incorporating where the action of the story takes place. If you use a Clarice Bean story, this could take the form of a road map. The children may find it helpful to identify the key features in the setting first, such as Clarice's house, Robert's house, her school and her street, listing them before they begin drawing. Help the children to fill in the 'gaps' left by the author, by drawing in places not mentioned in the story that would be likely to exist in 'real life', for example the local shops and a park.

❺ Use the maps to write a brief description of the community, perhaps for a local paper. For example, a report could be written entitled 'Wardour Street – the centre of our village', to include information about the architecture, people and landmarks, with a view of persuading people to the area. Or, in the case of *Six Dinner Sid*, the two streets can be contrasted through map-making and brief estate agents' reports.

## Moving on

● Encourage the children to use similar art techniques to that of Lauren Child by asking them to cut out pictures of houses, figures, cars and other things from magazines to make a collage effect.

● Consider asking the children to describe some of the places on their maps orally, then using this oral practice to write their own story. They could write it as another in the series of, for example, Clarice Bean stories, using the setting they have described and the key characters from the books, but introducing new incidents and the new places they have identified.

# Sorting the setting

This activity helps children to identify specific details of where stories are set and to begin to offer some descriptive vocabulary to establish the nature of the setting. It will enable them to categorise books by their settings and also help them as writers to construct and create settings for their own stories. The collaborative nature of the activity will support children firstly in articulating their interpretation of settings, from a potential range in the class book corner, and secondly, in determining where their own stories could be set. It will also generate a bank of vocabulary to inspire and challenge children as they write.

## What to do

❶ Brainstorm with the children all the texts they can remember that are set, for example, in one particular place – perhaps a bedroom. Consider texts such as *Where the Wild Things Are* by Maurice Sendak (Red Fox) and *Dear Greenpeace* by Simon James (Walker Books), which use the main character's bedroom for part of the story.

❷ Give the children an opportunity to browse through some of the books in the class library or book area to feed their repertoire of settings. Alternatively, give groups or pairs of children a box of books to search through. As they find a new

## Literature links

Stories such as *Cloudland* by John Burningham (Red Fox), *The Boy and the Cloth of Dreams* by Jenny Koralek (Walker Books) and *On the Way Home* by Jill Murphy (Macmillan), as well as Anthony Browne's work in several stories and *Beauty and the Beast* by Geraldine McCaughrean (Picture Corgi), offer clear, identifiable and mostly familiar settings. Using picture books at first will help children quickly categorise books according to setting, particularly if they are already familiar texts. However, moving on to extended texts with very clear settings, such as *Farm Boy* by Michael Morpurgo (HarperCollins), could help confident readers – and writers – draw on a wider range. Using texts with more ambiguous or more fluid settings, such as *The Dream Master* by Theresa Breslin (Yearling), which flits in space and time, or those that take place in more than one significant place, such as *Conker* by Michael Morpurgo (Mammoth), will begin to challenge the children to delve into the text to find descriptive vocabulary.

BEAUTY AND THE BEAST
Geraldine McCaughrean
Illustrated by
Gary Blythe

setting, add it to the class brainstorm-list until there is a major collection.

❸ Discuss the story settings the children have encountered, particularly those that are either ambiguous or exist in more than one place. Choose one of the most common or most interesting ones – such as a forest, home, school, the sea. Informally, create with the children a visual representation (for example, a frieze of winter woodland trees, quickly drawn with bold strokes), and ask the children to find book titles in their box or library area that have the same setting. Encourage them to write the titles on small pieces of paper or card and add these to the pictorial display.

❹ Provide pairs of children with strips of card to write on and ask them to think of evocative vocabulary (consider onomatopoeia and alliteration) to describe the setting. If you are looking at, for example, a fairy tale forest setting, you could give them examples from *Beauty and the Beast* by Geraldine McCaughrean (Picture Corgi): *a forest of fifty thousand trees, a sumptuous palace, lightless stairs*. If the children are copying from a book as well as writing their own cards, remind them to include the title and author on the card for reference.

❺ In a shared writing session, make use of the display and the vocabulary collected to write a descriptive paragraph about a place. Create the setting together, discussing and selecting the language from the collections. Begin to consider what might happen in this setting and who the reader might encounter, as this may influence the description.

❻ Include this shared paragraph as part of the display, as an example of a written description of a story setting.

© Chris Kelly

## Moving on

● Make the display interactive and ongoing so that children can continue to add book titles and vocabulary to the categories of setting identified. Encourage them to add new categories of setting as they encounter them in their reading. Ask them to find appropriate magazine and newspaper images and add these to the display to broaden the visual element.

● You could turn this into a word bank or writing resource, accessible to the children as they write their own stories. Book quotes and the children's own phrases could be collected in a pocket, pinned to the wall by the display or near the book corner so that the children can borrow from it and add to it.

● Identify possible characters that might be found in these settings and create new cards to list half a dozen characters for each setting. For example, in the wood the children might find goblins, deer, fairies, woodcutters, unicorns, wolves and so on. The pockets could be a valuable writing resource, offering two narrative elements to plan with.

# Compare and contrast

This activity aims to help children compare how different vocabulary works for different settings. Children are adept at understanding and 'reading' pictures. Much of their early engagement with stories will have involved pictures – in books, comics, television and film. This activity builds on that knowledge and uses it to engage the children in literacy learning. It encourages thoughtful writing, including turning pictures into words. The children start with oral composition suggestions, unfettered by the constraints of transcription. Once the ideas are down, they can begin to draft a complete piece of text. The activity is organised so that the children can share their ideas, building on each other's imaginations and constructing a text around this.

Albert Bierstadt – *Sierra Nevada Morning* © Corel

## Literature links

This activity is based on the examination of contrasting scenes. You may wish to draw on the rich range of children's book illustrators, like the work of Michael Foreman in Madhur Jaffrey's *Seasons of Splendour* (Puffin) or *The Brothers Grimm Popular Folk Tales* (Gollancz). Chris Riddell's work with Philip Ridley and in Kathryn Cave's *Something Else* (Puffin) and *Out for the Count* (Frances Lincoln) could also be used. Many text types have superb illustrators, but traditional tales seem to have them as a premium. Other examples include Joanna Troughton's *How Rabbit Stole the Fire* and

*Mufaro's Beautiful Daughters* by John Steptoe (both Puffin). Alternatively, you could use high-quality photographic images taken from colour newspaper supplements or magazines, or even quality travel brochures, or the work of painters from around the globe – both historical (works by Canaletto and Lowry include a wealth of detail, or work by the Impressionists) and contemporary (Andy Cook, Henderson Cisz, John Miller and Laurence Coulson create very atmospheric landscapes). Find some that are suitable for the kinds of stories you are reading and teaching about at the moment.

## What to do

**❶** You will need two contrasting images of settings. You may want to use a rural scene and an urban scene; or a frightening scene (thunder, lightning, gothic castles and so on) and a peaceful pastoral scene (sunshine, streams, country cottages); or perhaps you may prefer to focus on settings from different countries – Jamaica and England, for example. Collect a range of images that are interesting, perhaps 'busy' with the activities typical of the setting you wish to explore. Display any pair of contrasting evocative pictures that can be discussed and enjoyed as a class. One image should match the kind of settings found in the texts you are currently reading.

**❷** Ask the children to tell you what they perceive from the first picture in relation to their senses. They can work in pairs to discuss this and note their ideas on whiteboards. Encourage them to ask themselves questions such as: *What can I see? What would I hear? What would I smell? What might I feel? What might I taste?* When it comes to the 'feel' section, remind the children that it is not only referring to the physical sensations like temperature and perhaps grass beneath feet or the touch of tree bark or branches, but also the emotional sensations that different settings can evoke. Depending upon the experience of the children, you might want to model some ideas.

**❸** Share ideas for one setting, writing the most common or interesting on the board, then repeat the activity for the other picture.

**❹** Ask the children to remain working in pairs to compare and contrast their sensations from the two different pictures. Again, share these as a class and note them on the board.

**❺** Focus on the first picture again and use the children's ideas to model a descriptive paragraph of the setting. Welcome ideas from the children on how to structure the paragraph and which words and phrases will be effective. Model the thought processes of the writer as you go along. It will be a first draft, so you will need to model the mistakes and alterations that will always happen when setting out on a first draft.

**❻** Remind the children of the contrasts between the two settings, and perhaps brainstorm a few additional phrases for the second one. Then ask the children to work through the procedure you have followed to begin their own descriptive paragraphs for the second setting.

## Moving on

● Explain to the children that some descriptions of settings do not name the setting explicitly – they 'show' rather than 'tell'. The children could work in pairs to describe another pair of settings, based on another two pictures. Ask them to read through their notes and choose the setting that they find the most dramatic/exciting/comfortable/ frightening and so on, depending on the type of story they might be thinking of writing, and to work together to produce an evocative description. However, remind them not to name their setting in explicit terms – so, for example, they should avoid using words such as *seaside* or *forest* in their description. The children can then read their paragraph to the rest of the class who must try to work out which place the pair are describing.

● Ask the children to consider the impact on stories that settings have and to compare and contrast characters and events that might occur in the settings they have chosen. They should talk about, for example, who might live there, what they do, what will happen.

# Setting the comic scene

The purpose of this activity is to draw on children's knowledge of comics to discuss the importance of setting for stories. Using comics will motivate children to engage in the learning because their world of popular culture is brought into the classroom. For some reason, schools can neglect to draw on these popular interests that children often welcome in the classroom. The illustrators and writers of comics are experienced and skilled storytellers. Many of the techniques they use are the age-old techniques of storytelling in the way they structure the stories and set the scene. The illustrators and writers work together to make convincing short stories that many children read avidly. By studying these masters of the popular story children will learn a great deal and should be able to bring this knowledge to their own writing.

## What to do

❶ Choose one frame of a comic strip story that shows the setting of the story particularly well. Cut it out and position it into the centre of a large sheet of paper or, if you have the appropriate licence, transfer it onto acetate, so it can be annotated. Make similar sheets for the children to use.

© Chris Kelly

## Literature links

Today's children are still interested in the old favourite comics that we used to read, and the photo stories and comic strips found in modern children's magazines can also be used for this activity. Some struggling readers find comics a more accessible form of literacy, so you may be able to include ones that use a challenging reading level. Comics that accompany the computer-game world (for example *Sonic the Comic*) are often very similar to more obvious science fiction and fantasy texts, so this activity will work particularly well when studying these genres. *The Beano, The Dandy, Asterix, Tintin, Looney Tunes, Nickelodeon, Calvin and Hobbes* and Fox Kids' *Wickid* have their strips and stories set in a variety of places. Popular cultural texts like comics may not always be associated with traditional forms of story, but the settings in these stories serve the same functions as settings in more traditional formats – it is only the medium of storytelling that has changed.

❷ Show the comic strip story so that all the children can see it. Ask them to identify the setting. If the story moves across more than one setting, ask them to name each one. Encourage them to point out the evidence in the story to back up their examples. Then explain to the children that you are going to work together to adapt and elaborate on the setting shown in the comic strip to make it a setting for a written story.

❸ Ask the children to talk about the details of the place. It may be, for example, a futuristic, otherworldly landscape, with unusual rock formations, strange machinery or people, or it may be a fairly ordinary schoolroom or garden at home.

❹ Concentrate on the frame of the story you have chosen. Show and read it in its full context first, then introduce the prepared copy. Brainstorm words and phrases that describe the setting, noting the children's ideas all around the picture.

❺ Using these annotations, work together to compose a brief description of the setting in shared writing.

❻ Ask the children to work in pairs to annotate the frame and begin working on a paragraph to describe the picture. This is where you can encourage the children to enrich the comments they are giving. Push them to embellish their basic oral descriptions with words and phrases that suit a written description. Remind them to be aware of characters and events that might be influenced by the setting and to refer to these in their descriptions if appropriate.

## The Mystic Mountain

There was an massive, enormous, yellow fireball in the sky, spreading light across the desert. The While the Evil Emperor was showing his people round, two men on (arrived) camels arrived. They had been travelling for ages looking for water. The sand was very hot. It felt like a meteorite. The blue rock, home of the Genies, looked like a wrecked ship in the sand.

Page
**61**

## Moving on

● Ask pairs of children to note ideas for events and characters in a new story that happens in the comic strip setting you have examined. This could be the start of a story for the class collection perhaps. If it is a fantasy or science fiction setting the children will enjoy concocting strange and wondrous figures and situations.

● Consider asking the children, probably over a number of sessions, to draw and write their own comic strip story that happens in a setting of their choice. To achieve this, the children will have to use many of the devices of normal storytelling: setting, structure, characterisation, engaging beginnings, dramatic events and satisfactory endings. You could collate these to make a class comic.

# Predictions and parallels

In this activity, children speculate on the setting of a story by focusing on the title and any information they can gather from the book's cover. They will use prediction skills to explore the setting, drawing parallels with books they are already familiar with. This can build on work done in 'Zipped books' (page 10), using similar techniques but a different focus. The activity will support children in understanding the importance of a setting, and the way it is presented, in creating an enticing, believable world for the reader. This will enable them to draw on such understanding when creating their own stories with vivid settings.

## What to do

❶ Start off the activity by discussing the settings of a few familiar stories, identifying where in space and time the story begins, any journey undertaken, whether the story returns to the original setting at the end and so on. Use this opportunity to make links across texts, comparing books and the way in which stories develop, change, move from or return to particular places/settings.

## Literature links

The children will need to draw on their knowledge of a range of books from various genres for this activity, but for group work you will need to choose unfamiliar books with suggestive and comprehensive titles, for example *Beware of the Storybook Wolves* (Hodder) and *I will not ever never eat a tomato* (Orchard), both by Lauren Child, or *The Three Little Wolves and the Big Bad Pig* by Eugene Trivizas (Mammoth), which will also use the children's experience of traditional tales. An extended text could be *King Henry VIII's Shoes* by Karen Wallace (HarperCollins) or, for more experienced readers, *The Haunting* by Margaret Mahy (Puffin) might be a suitable challenge. It is important that these books for group work are *unknown* to the children.

❷ Following this initial discussion, organise the children into pairs and assign roles to individuals or pairs, giving them specific role cards. For example:
1. *I predict the main setting is going to be...*
2. *This is like/in direct contrast to...*

❸ Provide each pair of children with a book they have not seen before that has a provocative title and intriguing cover image and/or blurb. Each pair should have a different book. It is important that the book is not opened at this stage, so it might be a good idea to put it in a zipped plastic wallet to discourage children from opening it too quickly!

❹ Invite the pairs to work with their roles, making predictions about the setting and suggesting parallels with other texts that are similar to or very different from this text. Remind them that they are focusing on the setting, not character, structure or events in the story, although these considerations are likely to inform their ideas. The prompts work to help the children predict the setting and seek parallels in narratives they know.

❺ Ask the pairs to write a brief resumé of their setting predictions, drawing on evidence on the cover. Let them share these with other pairs and encourage comparisons across this range of books as well as stories the children already know. These predictions could then be displayed with copies of the books.

❻ Let the children look through and read the books to discover if their ideas coincide with those of the author. Discuss how illustrators provide clues on the front cover about the setting and, in some cases, the characters.

© Derek Cooknell

## Moving on

● Create an interactive display with book covers and questions set by the children, such as: *Where do you think this story opens?* and *How many different places do the characters encounter?* This could be an ongoing display, and might be used as a quiz at various points during the day.

● Ask the children to write a paragraph to set the scene of the story they have been speculating on. Encourage them to use their knowledge of texts with similar settings or texts by the same author, and to adopt an appropriate linguistic style. Remind them that their setting needs to create a picture in the mind's eye of the reader and be believable and precisely realised, whether fascinating and otherworldly or somewhere very familiar.

# Bringing the setting to life

This activity aims to enrich children's understanding of setting through improvisational involvement and reflection. They are involved initially in drawing, and then re-enacting a key scene or place in a narrative and as they do so, discuss, evoke and reflect upon the setting and its effect. The drama technique of freeze-frame or tableau (see page 22) is utilised here.

Atmosphere, which is an important element of a story's setting, can be created effectively through a sound collage and a physical re-creation of a place. This is a useful shared reading activity that can lead to writing that has greater clarity and more detail, as the children come to appreciate the three-dimensional quality and multi-sensory aspect of a setting.

## Literature links

Texts with a strong sense of place need to be selected, in which, for example, the barren landscape contributes to the desolation of the people. Michael Morpurgo's picture book *Blodin the Beast* (Frances Lincoln) is good for evoking the different physical terrains of the text. The Harry Potter novels work well for creating Diagon Alley, Dumbledore's office or one of the forest scenes, and can be enriched by the use of the films. Kevin Crossley-Holland's Arthur trilogy: *The Seeing Stone, At the Crossing Places* and *King of the Middle March,* (Dolphin) is centred in and around a real place – Caldecot – but at a time in the distant past, and also offers considerable potential for re-creation. You could also look at the stark contrasts in atmosphere in the different settings in CS Lewis's *The Lion, the Witch and the Wardrobe* (HarperCollins). At a less demanding level, *It's Too Frightening for Me* by Shirley Hughes (Puffin) is a short novel set in an eerie old house and is useful for bringing a setting's atmosphere to life.

## What to do

❶ Pause during the reading of your chosen text, at a moment when the setting has particular significance in the story. Explain that together you are going to 'fix' the place and evoke a sense of the setting.

❷ Invite the children to discuss in pairs what they see in their mind's eye from the descriptions you have just read. Share some of these with the class.

❸ Explain that initially you are going to draw the place, then re-create it. Draw on the board icons or simple pictures to represent a medieval market square, for example – inviting the children to contribute their ideas in words and pictures. The aim is to illustrate an agreed version of the place, whether this is a room, a cave, a town, or whatever – initially without people, but with the significant physical features shown. So in and around the market square, for example, there may be stalls, a town house or two, stocks, cobbles, a few trees, a cobbler's shop/stall, a blacksmith's, an ale house and so on.

❹ Next, briefly brainstorm and list the children's suggestions of the many people who might be present – the types of characters who are likely to populate this setting. For example, in the market place there might be traders; travellers selling posies, herbs and exotic goods; vagabonds in the stocks; children playing hoops; gentry wandering or riding through; the parson; a school master; drinkers in the alehouse; farmers or their wives selling their wares; other wives and servants shopping and so on.

❺ Invite each child to select one of the roles from the list, in discussion with their neighbour. Using the map or diagram drawn on the board to indicate positioning, ask the pairs to go to an appropriate place in the classroom and take up their roles. This improvisation will be uncertain at first; expect this and once you have helped the children to set themselves in position, take part yourself, circulating around in-role – perhaps as a gypsy selling heather.

❻ Once the pairs have settled into their roles, intervene to freeze the action. Move

© Chrs Kelly

around the scene, touching various individuals and inviting them to share who they are and what they are doing. For example: *I'm a mother, telling off my child for stealing an apple, I'm the landlord of the alehouse selling pints.*

7 Using a signal (such as a note from a tambourine or bells), bring the frozen tableaux back to life and let the children continue their improvisations, this time including movement and actions. Encourage the pairs to interact with other pairs nearby, as their characters would in the story.

8 Quickly invite out four children to observe the scene. Let them move around the edges, listening and quietly discussing in pairs what they can see.

9 Stop the improvisation and ask the four children to tell the others some of what they noticed.

10 Now move on to consider the various sounds that might also be heard in the scene. List some of the children's suggestions on the board. For example, church bells, maybe the town crier, horses' hooves, perhaps other livestock such as a cow or chickens, cart wheels over cobbles. Practise making the noises individually, then together. This will create a cacophony of possible sounds! Remind the children that conversations will be part of this too.

11 Briefly let the children continue their improvisations, including some of these noises and, particularly, dialogue. If appropriate, encourage them to use words and phrases that fit the time and place of the setting, such as *alehouse* instead of *pub*, or *master* instead of *teacher*.

12 Afterwards, ask the pairs to write a paragraph to describe the place. Prompt them to comment on the sights and sounds, even the smells, the atmosphere, the overheard conversations and other noises suggested earlier.

13 Share the children's descriptions. Reflect upon them and encourage the children to enrich them with reference to their class drawing and their improvisations.

© Chris Kelly

## Moving on

● Invite one group to re-create a mini-improvisation of particular relevance to the narrative and observe it together. The class could then describe the scene in detail through shared writing. Introduce more emphasis on narrative action in this writing and highlight the relationship between it and the setting.

● Help the children to notice the different settings in one story or chapter through each group representing a different one. These could be freeze-frames with sound collages to accompany and evoke them. For example, in *The Lion, the Witch and the Wardrobe* by CS Lewis, the crackling fire of Mr Tumnus's home contrasts with the cold winds and chill of Narnia by the lamp-post and the old empty house. In this example, children may well represent abstract objects or just create the sounds of the wind or children's voices echoing. These could then also be captured and elaborated on in descriptive paragraphs that include narrative action.

# Chapter Four

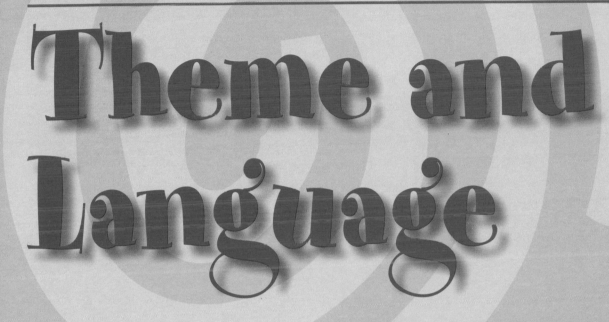

# Theme and Language

**Teachers need to use a range of open-ended activities to support young learners in exploring the themes of narratives and the language used to create narratives. Such activities endorse a multitude of possible responses to the story being studied and encourage children to engage with both meaning and vocabulary and to voice their feelings and views with reference to the text.**

## Theme

Exploring theme can be very rewarding as it encourages children to engage fully with the underlying meaning, essence and purpose of a story. Stories for children gain much of their richness from their strong themes, and they often contain messages and world views worth noting and discussing. Children need to understand that the theme is not the story, nor the events that take place, but the significance of those events to the characters and the world of the story.

To help their appreciation of this rather difficult concept, children of this age need to take part in activities that extend a story's theme through linking it to their own lives. In this way their understanding can be enriched and reinforced and they will connect with literature on a deeper level.

They may find it easier to discuss and reflect upon themes to write about than to compose texts of their own with a theme chosen for them, although problem resolution tales that

© Derek Cooknell

have one central dilemma or theme are more manageable to write. In these, a problem is articulated early in the narrative and the story seeks to examine the issues and consequences that this creates for the main character. For example, *A Baby for Grace* by Ian Whybrow (Kingfisher) is a picture book handling the tensions around the arrival of a new sister. The theme is clear throughout, shown in the visuals and through Grace's words and actions. This could be contrasted

with *Changes* by Anthony Browne (Walker Books), which examines the same theme. Continuing a theme like this in a story of their own encourages children to invent and connect to the sibling rivalry indicated in these books. Similarly, *You'll Soon Grow Into Them Titch* by Pat Hutchins (Red Fox) could be used and poetry, which can be highly focused on theme, could be read to supplement a focus on a particular theme.

Short stories (and picture books in particular) which encourage close observation are helpful for exploring themes. Stories written and illustrated by Anthony Browne, Philippe Dupasquier and Colin Thompson all offer strong evocations of theme. Identifying classic themes in traditional tales can also be a valuable starting point for young children, since such tales deal with archetypal issues about the human condition. These stories generally present a strong message in a clear and concise way, often incorporating contrasts. For example:

- from rags to riches
- the wise and the foolish
- the young and the old
- the quest to test
- the weak and the strong
- the beautiful and the ugly
- the journey as a symbol of self discovery.

These universal themes are not carried through the plot alone, but are invested in the characters, their development, the predicaments they face and in their life journeys. The metaphoric nature of the language of such texts also carries the theme, helping to create clearly contrasting characters whose motivations, behaviour, speech and feelings often highlight the themes in the text.

## Language

The language of stories, whether expressed in the first or third person, creates the tune on the page, the voice and the verve of the telling. The choice of vocabulary and style of language is important, so children need to hear, read, study and experience a wide range of such voices. Focusing on a particularly prolific author (such as Jacqueline Wilson, Michael Morpurgo, Dick King-Smith, Chris Powling or Berlie Doherty) across a unit of work will encourage children to read examples themselves and examine an author's style.

Traditional tales are again a particularly valuable resource for studying story language, as they often have distinctive language patterns marked by repetitive and memorable vocabulary, attached to often repetitive events and conversations. Such language often abounds with metaphor and imagery. 'Standard' openings and endings as well as rhythmic refrains and repeated phrases are common in this genre and help an experienced reader to know what to expect from the story. This in turn makes the reader's access to and involvement in stories more comfortable and fulfilling.

Many traditional tales were originally intended to be spoken and heard, remembered and retold, and those with a strong oral orientation, even in modernised and subverted versions, still retain strong elements of rhythm, resonance and repetition. Some written versions of oral tales retain a direct and lively language, while others incorporate a poetic, lyrical, more complex and 'textual' style.

There is a wealth of modern versions of traditional tales, so the opportunity to compare and contrast the styles and tones of language is readily available.

**Some particularly powerful picture book retellings in which the language sings and the literary style is well worth enjoying, alongside fabulous illustrations, are listed *right*. These texts also make clear their themes, to which many personal connections can be made. Suggestions for other suitable texts are given in the 'Literature links' sections of each of the activities described in this chapter.**

- *Blodin the Beast* – Michael Morpurgo (Frances Lincoln)
- *The Wise Doll* – Hiawyn Oram (Red Fox)
- *Mufaro's Beautiful Daughters* – John Steptoe (Puffin)
- *Brother Eagle, Sister Sky* – Susan Jeffers (Puffin)
- *The Little Match Girl* – Hans Christian Andersen, illustrated by Rachel Isadora (GP Putnam)
- *The Twelve Dancing Princesses* – the brothers Grimm, illustrated by Jane Ray (Orchard)
- *Nobody Rides The Unicorn* – Adrian Mitchell (Picture Corgi)
- *The Emperor's New Clothes* – translated by Naomi Lewis (Walker Books)
- *Beauty and the Beast* – Geraldine McCaughrean (Picture Corgi)

# Monuments

This activity aims to actively and physically engage the children in representing the theme of a story in the form of a group monument or 'mimed' sculpture. This will involve the children in valuable group discussion about the theme of the story, and invites them to creatively capture it. Together they seek to agree a way of presenting the theme with their bodies, either literally or in a more abstract manner. The concrete nature of their representation and the discussion that leads to it helps children connect personally to the theme and make greater sense of it.

## What to do

❶ Complete the first reading of a picture book, short story or novel (or revisit a recently read text) that has a complex and interesting theme.

❷ After reading, ask the children to work in pairs to discuss the many layers of meaning they noticed in the story. For example, ask: *What message is the writer trying to convey? What points of view or positions/stances is he or she exploring? What are the important events in the story?* And from this, it is important to ask: *Why are they important?*

❸ Don't take class feedback now; instead re-organise the children into groups of four or five. Explain that they are going to position themselves to make a monument or sculpture that might have been erected in memory of one of the characters or to commemorate the events of the tale. For example, in 'The Willow Pattern Story', Koong-Se's father might have had a memorial built to show that he was sorry and had learned his lesson. Or, in *Rose*

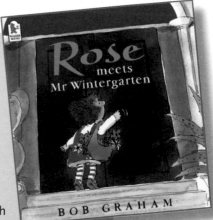

## Literature links

This activity works well with challenging picture book fiction in which the theme is not necessarily obvious or simple. For example:

● *Rose Meets Mr Wintergarten* – Bob Graham (Walker Books)
● *Angus Rides the Goods Train* – Alan Durrant (Picture Corgi)
● *The Tunnel* – Anthony Browne (Walker Books)
● *The Snow Queen* – Hans Christian Anderson, illustrated by PJ Lynch (Red Fox)
● *Watch Out, Fred's About!* – Catherine Sefton (Puffin)
● *The Clothes Horse and Other Stories* – Allan Ahlberg (Viking Kestrel)
● 'The Willow Pattern Story' (page 84).

All these texts are multi-layered and need to be examined at some length. Your current class read could also be used as, even if it is a long story, the children will know it well enough to be able to discuss its central themes and issues. This activity encourages an engaging response to a text and generates a shared reading of meaning and message.

*Meets Mr Wintergarten* by Bob Graham, perhaps the old gentleman, now friends with his neighbours, has a sculpture placed in his garden to symbolise his journey from darkness to light. Encourage the children to avoid showing actual characters from the story, as the monument will be there for all time, but to convey the message of the text.

❹ Model how to achieve this with your classroom assistant and/or a couple of children, showing one or two instant pieces of human sculpture. For example, Mr Wintergarten might have made a sundial with a posy of stone flowers at its base to recall Rose's flowers and his opening up to the world. Or you could make a statue with one person crouched down, head covered, representing the dark and lonely part of his life, and one standing up, arms outstretched, welcoming warmth and friendship.

❺ After discussion and rehearsal, prompt presentation of the sculptures. Make it clear to the children there are no 'right answers', only their interpretation of the story. Remind them that their monument could be abstract. For example, Mr Wintergarten's past and future could be represented as two sides of the same shape. Let the children adjust their shapes if they wish.

❻ Comment on a couple of the sculptures, then ask each group to title their sculpture, giving it a clever, subtle name that hints at the theme represented rather than states it explicitly. This will focus discussion on the theme.

❼ As a class, observe each monument, perhaps letting the children suggest titles for other group's monuments and discuss the possible theme shown, *before* the titles are decided.

❽ Ask the groups or individuals to write a short dedication that may have been inscribed at the base of the monument, or an information plaque put up next to it. Advise the children to use whatever idea suits their interpretation of the story.

© Derek Cooknell

❾ Ask the children to re-create their monuments, and share the paragraphs as you observe the monuments for the last time. You may want to take photographs, as they can form a focused and interesting display alongside the plaques.

## Moving on

● Ask the groups to let each of their members step out of the monument in turn, observe it as a director and suggest a small improvement. Encourage them to feed such refinements into their written work.

● Suggest to the children that they imagine their monument is to be constructed. Consider materials for the monument to be made from – such as wire, steel, bronze, cotton wool, bark, stone and so on. Encourage them to think of this material in terms of the theme, adding another dimension to the monument's nature: endurance, security, fragility. For example, a Mr Wintergarten monument might be made out of steel to suggest the permanence of the lesson he had learned, but with a container for fresh flowers that denotes new life.

# Re-title the tale

**The purpose of this activity is to help children understand how titles can suggest the content of the book and indicate its tone and genre. This activity will also help children to assess, analyse and summarise content and to use linguistic devices such as alliteration, rhyme or onomatopoeia in their own story titles.**

## Literature links

Picture books could include *The Story of the Little Mole Who Knew It Was None of His Business* by Werner Holzwarth (HarperCollins) or *M.O.L.E* by Russell Hoban (Red Fox). Extended texts could include one of the Horrid Henry books by Francesca Simon, *Harold the Hairiest Man* by Laurence Anholt (Orchard), *Krazy Kow Saves the World – Well, Almost* by Jeremy Strong (Puffin) or versions of traditional tales, such as 'The Willow Pattern Story' (page 84) or 'Anansi and Postman Snake' (page 94).

## What to do

❶ Spread out a selection of books on the children's tables, comprising familiar texts that have interesting or suggestive titles.

❷ Let the children look through the display; then pick out one or two books as examples to focus on. Discuss the title and the story text with the children, emphasising the connections between, for example, the humour in the title and humour in the book, the ambiguity of the title or the potential for subversion.

❸ Invite the children, in pairs, to select a text that they know well. Provide time for discussion about the title and the content.

Ask the children to experiment with their own titles for the book, choosing an alternative device that still highlights the theme. For example, Lauren Child's *I will not ever never eat a tomato* could be turned into *Tempting Toddlers to Taste Tomatoes* or *You Can't Make Me Eat It*; Eugene Trivizas' *The Three Little Wolves and the Big Bad Pig* could be re-titled as *Wolves: 3, Pig: 1* or *Let's Swap Places*.

❹ Give the children strips of card on which to present their new book titles.

❺ Provide an opportunity for the children to share and display their ideas, focusing discussion on their use of linguistic devices, such as onomatopoeia and plays on words, as well as clues to the content.

## Moving on

● Ask the children to write a blurb to go with their new book titles, justifying their choices of what they include and how it is written with reference to the theme of the text.

● Encourage the children to construct guessing games, matching new titles with the original books.

● Let the children create titles for sequels or prequels of favourite books or films.

# Represent the story

In this activity, children consolidate their understanding of the key elements that comprise the essence and meaning of a story. The activity will also help them to develop their personal responses to stories.

## Literature links

Texts that suggest clear representational and physical images to the children are best for this activity. Both picture books and longer stories could be used. You could choose any of the 'Stories to Tell' from page 83, or other suggestions are:

- *Six Dinner Sid* – Inga Moore (Macdonald Young Books)
- *The Owl Who Was Afraid of the Dark* – Jill Tomlinson (Mammoth)
- *Weslandia* – Paul Fleischman (Walker Books)
- *The Little Boat* – Kathy Henderson (Walker Books).

## What to do

❶ Read the chosen story to the children. Ask them to record key words or images that present themselves during the reading.

❷ Ask the children what the theme or central issue in the story might be. This could be a brainstorming session in which children remember significant events, the presentation of ideas and views – all of which combine to present the theme. The vocabulary or images gathered could then be categorised into specific themes such as bullying, fear, loss, adventure, old and young, power and so on.

❸ Ask the children to work individually or in pairs to record an image, perhaps combined with a word or phrase, that they believe represents the central theme of the story. For example, *Six Dinner Sid* could be shown as two separate streets with Sid in between, reflecting how the first street of owners did not talk to each other and became jealous of Sid's other 'owners', whereas when Sid moves to Aristotle Street, the owners talk to each other and are happy to share Sid. Share the children's ideas.

❹ In pairs or groups of four, ask the children to select a book and represent it on A3 paper, either through the use of a single picture, containing detail to represent the theme, or by a number of pictures that highlight the theme in some way. Display and share these visual representations.

❺ The children could write summaries of their representations to accompany their designs, as in a gallery.

## Moving on

- As an independent activity, you could provide the children with blank cards (the size of playing cards) so that they can create a visual image on one side and write the title on the other, in order to creating a guessing card game.

# Puzzle possibilities

This activity aims to support children in focusing on the language of written stories. It is based on Aidan Chambers' strategy for discussing text: Like, Dislike, Puzzle, Pattern detailed in *Book Talk* (Thimble Press). The puzzle possibility game/activity is a development of this, which encourages children to articulate their understanding of particular phrases, lines of dialogue or longer passages from a text and to support this comprehension with reference to the rest of the text. The activity also helps children appreciate alternative readings and other possible responses. From that they will gain understanding of how authors choose the language they use very carefully in order to achieve certain effects. The activity is useful in both shared and guided reading when a complex text deserves close examination and requires reading beyond the literal.

## What to do

❶ Select a passage from a current text. Ensure the passage contains language relevant to your focus – for example, a character description, contrasting evocations of places, a sensual description of a setting or a dramatic, pacy build-up and moment of tension in the text.

❷ Word-process enough copies of the passage for pairs or individuals, allowing sufficient space around the text for the children's annotations. A3 is the most useful size for this, with the selected text placed in the centre of the page.

❸ Remind the children of the story you are reading, then re-read enough of the preceding text and the actual passage itself to help position the passage in the narrative. Avoid giving it straight out to the class as cold text. By reading part of

## Literature links

Passages from a novel the class is reading or havs recently read will work well for this activity, as the children will bring a wide knowledge of the text and its characters to the discussions. The often metaphoric but succinct and powerful language of poetry is also useful, as the activity seeks to challenge the sometimes literal interpretation of texts given by children. The vivid literary language in the following suggested books can help

highlight the complexity and power of rich literary language:

● *The Dancing Bear* – Michael Morpurgo (Lions)
● *Willa and Old Miss Annie* – Berlie Doherty (Walker Books)
● *Beauty and the Beast* – Geraldine McGaughrean (Picture Corgi)
● *Mr Bear and the Bear* – Frances Thomas (Andersen Press).

the run-up to this passage, the plot, narrative power and language will begin to interest and involve the children.

❹ Invite the children to consider in pairs what they like and dislike about the passage. For example, do they like particular words or phrases, and why? Are these evocative, helping them see pictures in their minds? Do they like a particular character because he reminds them of a friend? How is that character described? What does he say? Perhaps the children dislike a particular paragraph as it makes them feel afraid or confused.

❺ Allow the children to share a few examples, but try to avoid sharing your own views at this stage, as the children may perceive these are the 'right answers'.

❻ Give out the A3 copies and attach one to the flipchart. Model the process of recording likes and dislikes by writing one or two of the children's views in the margins on the flipchart copy.

❼ Ask the children to record their views around their copies of the text, recording a couple of elements they like and a couple they dislike, perhaps with simple bullet points. Remind them to include reasons for their opinions and refer directly to the text – for example, by underlining or drawing key lines.

❽ Share the children's annotations and challenge the class to identify patterns and puzzles they can see in the text. The patterns may be in any form, such as rhymes, repetitions, contrasts, parallels, alliterative phrases and patterned language to stress the meaning. The puzzles, in effect, are aspects of the language, interpretation or meaning that are not fully understood. Let the children discuss these further with one another.

❾ Through whole-class discussion, share a puzzle and ponder possible explanations together. One puzzle will proliferate many possibilities, as you offer possible responses (not 'answers'). Encourage the children offering explanations to refer to the text and talk through their thoughts. Stress throughout that as readers we respond differently to aspects of literary language. There are no rights and wrongs; we are not all 'puzzled' by the same points, but opinions and perspectives can often be explained with reference to other parts or other aspects of the text and to our lives.

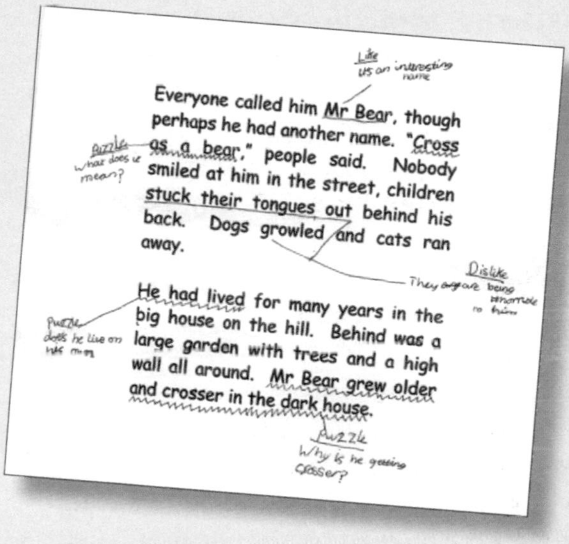

Handwritten annotations on the text:

Like
is an interesting name

Everyone called him Mr Bear, though perhaps he had another name. "Cross as a bear," people said. Nobody smiled at him in the street, children stuck their tongues out behind his back. Dogs growled and cats ran away.

Puzzle
what does it mean?

Dislike
They are being horrible to him

He had lived for many years in the big house on the hill. Behind was a large garden with trees and a high wall all around. Mr Bear grew older and crosser in the dark house.

Puzzle
does he live on his own?

Puzzle
Why is he getting crosser?

## Moving on

● Record the puzzles on the board and bullet-point possible responses in note form. Then one or two puzzle possibilities could be written up as a summary of your shared reading.

● Pairs could create puzzles for others, and several possible responses will be recorded as the sheets travel around the class. These can be initialled by those responding and shared with the class in a plenary. This will involve them in noting genuine puzzles in the text and challenging other pairs to explain them.

● A display sharing such puzzles and possibilities helpfully reminds children of the variety of reader responses, supported by reference to the text.

# Traditional themes

**In this activity, children identify themes, patterns, structures and characters conventionally used in traditional tales. The activity will help children to draw on this understanding for use in their own written stories. The popularity and longevity of such tales gives an indication of how clearly their messages are conveyed. They are ideal texts for exploring the story element of theme.**

## What to do

❶ Read or retell a traditional tale, such as 'Snow White'. Identify the themes that emerge from it (for example, good versus evil) and discuss how these have been personified by the two main characters: Snow White and her stepmother.

❷ Explore with the children other familiar traditional tales, looking at the same theme in those tales and identifying other themes. For example, in 'Beauty and the Beast', the theme focuses on beauty being more than skin deep: the 'ugly' beast is a caring individual. This is similar to 'Snow White', in which the beautiful queen is ugly and wicked inside.

❸ Ask the children in pairs to select a story of their own. Distribute strips of card to write individual themes that emerge from their text. Using some of their ideas, such as rags to riches from 'Cinderella', identify other traditional tales or known stories that include a similar theme. Discuss how similar themes, patterns of events and character types recur in such tales.

### Literature links

It may be important to work only with conventional tellings of traditional tales, such as 'Hansel and Gretel', 'Snow White', 'Beauty and the Beast' or 'Cinderella'. 'The Willow Pattern Story' (page 84), 'Little River Turtle' (page 88), 'The Rajah's Big Ears' (page 91) and 'Anansi and Postman Snake' (page 94) could all be used effectively in this activity.

### Moving on

● Identify characters who demonstrate elements of themes (for example, wickedness) and create categories of characters from traditional tales on a wall display. You could include characters that display jealousy, such as the stepmother in 'Snow White', or characters that show goodness, generosity and kindness, such as Snow White herself.

● This activity could be developed by exploring traditional texts and challenging the children to identify vocabulary that indicates a wicked, jealous or greedy character and so on. Highlight particular words or phrases to collect in a word bank to support the children's development and melding together of theme and character and the use of language in their own writing.

# Quote and comment

This activity encourages children to use their reading journals effectively – to record, review and comment on texts they encounter and to quote their favourite passages. It provides an opportunity and an audience for them to articulate their views about particular books and encourages them to speak and write persuasively about them. In quoting from texts and justifying their views, children will be paying close attention to the text and noticing significant language. Over time, this will contribute to their written work.

## What to do

❶ Select an extract from your own reading – whether adult or children's literature – to read to the children. Explain why you like the piece you have chosen.

❷ Ask the children to select an extract from their reading, that they particularly like. They could do this during the lesson or beforehand, perhaps for homework.

❸ Focus on a particular quote from your chosen passage and record it on the board. Explain to the children why you chose this phrase/sentence/line of dialogue/brief description. Record your reasons in writing, making reference to the text.

❹ Following your explanation of why you chose the quote you did, encourage the children to share their extract in conversation with a partner, giving details about why they chose it and referring to specific parts of the text.

❺ Ask the children to select and copy their own quote into their reading journal.

❻ Pool the reasons for the children's choices. Celebrate the diversity and help the children understand that readers are not the same: each person looks for different things in texts and responds differently to the same things.

## Literature links

This activity makes use of a range of texts available in the classroom, since the children will be using their own reading books – perhaps old favourites they have brought in from home.

## Moving on

● In guided reading, in the company of others who have also read the same text, children can develop the habit of articulating their views and being prepared to offer direct reference to the text in support of them.

● Encourage the children to create a picture to accompany their quote to help them convey the visual image created by the description, or the feeling evoked by the language.

# Word walls

This activity focuses explicitly on the language of stories and through it children can, over time, develop their knowledge about language use and their awareness of an author's chosen vocabulary. Their interest in words and their meanings can be developed. Through discussion they can be taught to notice the subtle distinctions between words with similar meanings, and to experiment with choices of vocabulary. A word wall can be undertaken during or after reading a particular story. The idea is not to fill in each brick in the wall, but rather to identify particularly interesting or powerful words and phrases that enrich the text. These are then discussed, their use and role explored, and they are recorded in the wall.

## What to do

❶ Create a word wall similar to the example *right*, which offers bricks for children to record words or phrases from the story that are in some way noticeable. You could make one as an A3 laminated poster, or make a 'real' word wall with cut-out paper bricks of different colours, or just create an instant word wall on the board. You will also need smaller copies of the word wall for the children and several paragraphs from the second half of a story as examples.

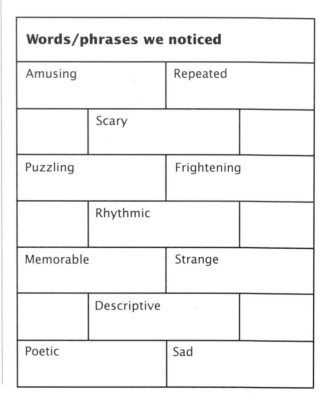

| Words/phrases we noticed | | | |
|---|---|---|---|
| Amusing | | Repeated | |
| | Scary | | |
| Puzzling | | Frightening | |
| | Rhythmic | | |
| Memorable | | Strange | |
| | Descriptive | | |
| Poetic | | Sad | |

## Literature links

Stories with rich, literary, 'wordy' language is not a necessity for this activity, since simply told tales can also contain evocative phrases, powerful word choices, highly distinctive lines and memorable dialogue or descriptions. Picture books, which often make very 'efficient' use of language, are also appropriate. It is also possible to create word walls specifically for particular authors to help ascertain their style, for example, when comparing short stories in collections such as:

- *From Hereabout Hill* – Michael Morpurgo (Mammoth)
- *Counting Stars* – David Almond (Hodder)
- *The Rope and Other Stories* – Philippa Pearce (Puffin)
- *Freaky Tales from Far and Wide* – Hugh Lupton (Barefoot Books).

The tales contained in the 'Stories to Tell' chapter at the end of this book could also be used for this purpose.

❷ Read a selected short story or picture book once, stopping to discuss the meaning, events and characters (not the language) at various points, as you would normally.

❸ Now explain to the children that you want them to help you record the noticeable language of the story you have just read. Present this as a kind of game and show them the large word wall.

❹ Then re-read the first part of the narrative, pausing after every couple of paragraphs or sections, to allow the children to record any distinctive or repeating language they notice. They could do this on whiteboards. Stress there is no right answer, as we all respond differently to different language and different stories.

❺ Share the children's recordings, and write any noticeable phrases, sentences or words that they recorded on a suitable brick in the wall, using any unlabelled bricks to create new categories. Discuss the language the children have noted. Why do they think the author chose these phrases – what effect do they have? The idea here is not to discuss each word, but to seize on three or four to reflect upon together.

❻ Provide word-processed copies of the next few paragraphs of the text. Let the children read these for themselves and select some language to record on their own copies of the word wall.

❼ Share some selected examples and ask the children to justify their selection and its position on the word wall. Synonyms (or different phrases similar in meaning) could be recorded in a particular colour on the wall, and through use of thesauruses, alternative words very similar in meaning could be identified and discussed.

## Moving on

● The children could work in pairs to read each other's work and select particularly powerful, memorable and noticeable language to include in a word wall. This exercise acts as a commentary on the language aspect of the children's writing and can be shared with everyone or included on the whole-class word wall. It may be useful to model it with one child's work first.

● As they read their current reading books, prompt the children to record noticeable language in their reading journals, commenting on why they selected this passage or phrase, how it makes the reader feel and how this effect is achieved. This word focus in their reading journals could be occasional and is also useful in relation to poetry, advertisements and newspaper reports. In effect, the bricks and wall have been removed but the development and learning is essentially the same.

● After quiet reading time, you could ask the children to select a phrase from their book to read aloud to their partner and explain why they like it. This is a kind of oral word wall.

# Shaping and polishing

This activity is useful during or after writing to help children make decisions about a piece of writing and make changes that improve the quality of the piece. It will involve the children thinking about the audience and purpose for the writing, connecting to relevant literature they have read in that genre. Working with response partners, the children seek to improve a particular piece of writing, and this practice will inform other writing tasks they are involved in. When children are engaged in an extended piece of writing that will be published in some form, they need time to reflect on its qualities, particularly in terms of its composition and effect and adaptation according to purpose and audience. Like all writers, children are often reluctant to edit, rewrite and change a piece that is being worked on. This is why it is very important that they have the opportunity to write for real audiences.

### Literature links

This activity works well within any unit of work around a text type where the children are asked to write within a particular genre, for a particular purpose or to 'imitate' the style of an author. The work of many significant children's writers could be focused on, including Dick King-Smith, Jacqueline Wilson, Michael Morpurgo, Jeremy Strong, Berlie Doherty and Philippa Pearce.

The readership maybe their peers for a chapter in the growing class novel; it may be a letter to a football team fan club, or a poem for a school anthology and so on. If the writing is always for an exercise book that is stored in their tray where nobody sees it, much of the motivation for communicating through writing will be lost. Conversely, it is also important to remember that not all the writing done at school is perfected, shaped and polished. Some of the children's written work will involve note-taking or writing personal journals and diaries, for which the kind of shaping and polishing suggested here is not helpful or appropriate. It would be necessary to model the shaping and polishing process for the children before they attempt it independently. This can be done as a shared writing session or as guided writing, as described in 'Moving on' on page 82. Ask the permission of a child to use his/her work when modelling how to provide the advice of a 'critical' friend in these shared sessions. Children need considerable support to build up their response partnership skills – generic comments such as *It's lovely* or *I like it* are unfocused and unhelpful. You may wish them to relate their comments to the learning objective, the purpose of the writing, or to their engagement as a reader. Children will take time to develop their response skills, but these skills will enrich the shaping and polishing of their writing.

## What to do

❶ When the children have completed a first draft of a piece of writing, ask them to work in pairs to discuss, shape and polish the work they have been involved with individually. Explain to them that they should swap the work they have been doing and let their partners read through their work.

❷ They should then discuss, in the first instance, two things they like about the piece – taking into consideration the audience, purpose and learning objective – and two recommendations for ways of improving the piece. For example, although the work begins to successfully describe a funny character, the reader may need more description, or perhaps more *precise* description, in order to see the person in his or her mind's eye. These comments could be written on the child's work as areas of success and areas of development, and signed by the response partner who made them. Explain to the children that, as discussed below, these are comments on the first draft when the children need to focus on composition rather than transcription. Spelling, grammar and punctuation could be the focus for shaping and polishing at a later stage of the writing and redrafting process.

❸ Give the children time to work together to improve each other's writing until they feel satisfied and proud of their work. This may well involve asterisks, arrowed additions, crossing out and considerable rephrasing.

❹ If there is time, turn one of the children's pieces into an overhead transparency and focus on it as a class. Ask the writer to offer his or her comments, then discuss responses to the piece, before finally revealing the response partner's shaping and polishing ideas.

❺ Alternatively, tell the pairs to join with other pairs to make groups of four, and read out and comment on each other's writing, discussing in particular the improvements made and the new ideas expressed. This will help the children to value their response partners. Hearing their work read aloud also helps them to appreciate aspects of their work that they may not have noticed before.

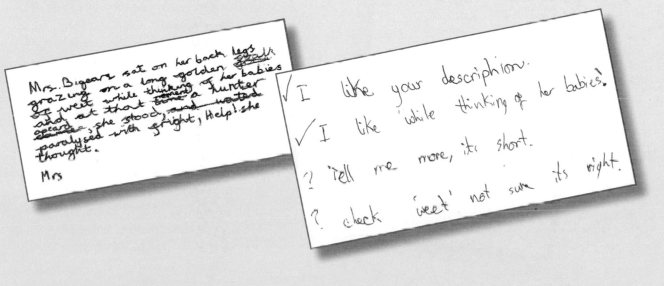

❻ It may be useful to make a clean copy now or use a computer to reshape this work. The children could also be set the shaping task for homework, acting on their response partner's advice.

❼ In a plenary or whole-class discussion, ask the children to read comparable extracts from both their previously unpolished and now shining work. Focus together as a class on the ways in which the new piece has been improved – for example, its greater clarity, richer description, or a new conciseness that shines forth. You could write some of the extracts on the board or copy them onto an OHT for more fruitful comparison.

❽ Publishing the children's work in class could also involve producing a wall display that graphically demonstrates the process of changing, exchanging, shaping and polishing writing that the children have been through. Such a display reminds the writers of the ongoing, reflective and self-critical business of working on their writing.

## Moving on

● Consider using this activity in a guided writing session where, with the permission of the child, you lead a discussion about how to shape and polish a piece of work in progress. You may find the children seem convinced that they must concentrate on the spelling, punctuation and handwriting rather than the meaning and language of the piece and its appropriateness for the chosen audience.

● Give your shaping and polishing periods a clear focus for what is to be critiqued. This should be related to what part of the writing process the children have reached (planning, drafting, editing, proofreading or publication). So, for example, it would not be appropriate for the children to be correcting spelling during the time they are drafting a composition. We know from research that concentrating on both composition and transcription simultaneously impedes the progress of each. When teachers emphasise the writing process, the children, like professional writers, can focus on each part separately. The shaping and polishing process can reflect this progression.

● Invite professional writers who can also be encouraged to share their drafts with the children to demonstrate the complex process of moving from reading through talking to writing.

# Stories to Tell

# The Willow Pattern Story

Once, many years ago, there lived a rich mandarin. The mandarin's daughter Koong-Se had fallen in love with one of his servants, Chang. The young couple adored one another and stole precious moments together whenever they could. They knew that the mandarin would be outraged if he found out, for their positions in life were unequal and the mandarin would never have consented to their union. Koong-Se and Chang met under the privacy of the willow trees by day or in the darkness of the gardens by night. There they would tell tales of their childhoods, share songs and secrets together and whisper their hopes for the future.

One day, however, they were discovered. The mandarin, in his fury, forbade his daughter to go beyond the bounds of the house and had a high wall built to prevent Chang getting in. As well as being a prisoner in her own home, Koong-Se was betrothed to a wealthy ta-jin, or duke, whom she had never seen. He was an old man who had never married. A nuptial date was agreed for the ta-jin and Koong-Se: when the peach tree blossomed in the spring, they were to be wed.

Poor Koong-Se was bereft without her beloved, and she dreaded the impending marriage. She felt all alone in the world. Yet Chang did not desert her, and sent tame birds to her fortress home with messages of love and hope. The lovers also floated endearments to one another in a little coconut shell with a tiny cloth sail.

But time was passing and as the buds on the peach tree began to form, fear filtered through the fronds of the willow tree and entered Koong-Se's heart. The ta-jin sent food and wine in advance of the wedding feast and came to visit the mandarin with a gift of precious jewels as a dowry for his daughter. Servants bore the old man on a sedan chair and a reception was held in his honour. The two men drank too many cups of celebration and salutation, so they didn't notice a small figure who slipped into the house. It was Chang. He sought out his beloved and seized the box of jewels, and together they escaped from the house and ran across the bridge to freedom. They were soon followed in fury by the mandarin who raised a hue and cry and demanded that servants rescue his errant daughter and kill the lover thief.

But the pair had escaped and found a safe home in which to dwell away from prying eyes. The little house belonged to the mandarin's gardener. For a while the couple were very happy there. They even married in secret and exchanged rings.

The mandarin, with murder in his heart, continued to search for them. Eventually, suspicion fell upon the gardener, and guards were sent to search his house. The couple, protected by the wit and willing of the gardener's wife, just had time to secure a tiny boat and set sail in the waters, taking the jewels with them.

In the grey light of morning, the little craft entered the Yangtze river and the couple needed all their skills to stay afloat in its rushing current. But this they did, finally coming to ground upon a tiny reed island in the middle of the broad river. The young couple decided to settle down here and live the rest of their days in peace and harmony.

Inconspicuously they sold the jewels and together they built a home and cultivated the land. Many years later, Chang wrote a book about agriculture, reflecting upon what they had learned in reclaiming their island of reeds.

The success of Chang's book, however, exacted a terrible toll upon the couple for it revealed their whereabouts to the ta-jin who still carried revenge in his heart. He attacked the island and showed Chang no mercy, and Koong-Se, in despair, set alight to their home and perished in the flames. The gods took pity on the couple whose constancy and love for one another had never wavered. They transformed them into two immortal doves who could dwell together forever in the world above.

# The Tailor's Button

Many many years ago, in the court of a great queen, there lived a tailor of considerable repute. He was a shy man, quiet of manner and of mind, but a quite brilliant tailor whose seams were almost invisible and whose skills were known all around the court.

One day, an extraordinary bolt of silk arrived for the queen, a gift from a Chinese admirer. It was an iridescent blue which, when partially unrolled, revealed peacocks, parrots and macaws strutting across its surface. When the cloth was completely unrolled, rare beasts of the land, birds of the air and fish of the sea could be seen woven into its silken skin. All the colours of the rainbow seemed to gleam and glitter from the cloth.

The tailor was instructed to make the queen a ball gown, the like of which had never been seen. He put all his skills to good effect, and the queen was indeed the belle of the ball in the fabulous creation the tailor had made for her. When she danced it seemed as if the birds and butterflies in the cloth were dancing too.

When the tailor respectfully enquired what Her Majesty would have him do with the remaining material, she generously bestowed it upon him, declaring that her beautiful ball gown was all she desired.

That very same night, by candlelight, the tailor snipped and clipped the gorgeous cloth. He snipped and he clipped, and he stitched and he sewed. He stitched and he sewed until he had fashioned a jacket, and a very fine and colourful jacket it was.

Whenever the tailor wore the jacket he felt *goood* about himself; so very *goood* about himself in fact that he began to lose some of his shyness, holding his head high and looking around with more confidence and joie de vivre.

But as time passed, the tailor's jacket grew thin and worn, and he had to cut down the jacket to save what he could of the special cloth.

So, by candlelight, he snipped and he clipped, he snipped and he clipped, and he stitched and he sewed. He stitched and he sewed until he had fashioned a waistcoat. A dapper little waistcoat it was indeed, with slanting pockets and neat pin tucks.

Whenever the tailor wore the waistcoat, he felt *goood* about himself; so very *goood* about himself in fact that, as he smoothed his waistcoat, he would look towards the ladies of the court and wonder…

But as time passed, the tailor's waistcoat grew grubby from such constant smoothing and so much wear.

So, by candlelight, he snipped and he clipped, he snipped and he clipped, and he stitched and he sewed. He stitched and he sewed until he'd fashioned himself a cravat. A large, floppy, shimmering cravat it was indeed, which he wore tied in a splendid bow around his neck.

Whenever the tailor wore the cravat he felt *goood* about himself; so very *goood* about himself in fact that he began to converse with the ladies, delicately touching his cravat for confidence as he did so.

Time continued to pass, as it is wont to do, and with so much tender touching of his cravat, the ends grew frayed and frail.

So, by candlelight, the tailor snipped and he clipped, he snipped and he clipped, and he stitched and he sewed, he stitched and he sewed until he'd fashioned himself a hatband. It wasn't a very wide hatband, but it was brilliant blue and gleaming nonetheless.

Whenever the tailor wore his hat with the beautiful hatband, he felt *goood* about himself; so very *goood* about himself in fact that he began to spend quite a bit of time with one lady in particular. He wore his hat so often, she began to wonder what he would look like without it!

However, the hatband too began to wear out.

So, by candlelight, after much snipping and clipping, stitching and sewing, the tailor fashioned himself a small handkerchief, on which the tail feathers of a peacock could be seen.

Whenever he wore that handkerchief, tucked into his tailcoat pocket, well, the tailor felt *goood* about himself; so very *goood* about himself in fact that he even proposed to his young lady. And she accepted!

On the night before they were wed, the tailor sat up late, and by candlelight, he snipped and he clipped, he snipped and he clipped, and he stitched and he sewed, he stitched and he sewed, and finally fashioned himself a button, a beautiful azure blue silk button which he wore on his wedding day. Oh, he felt *goood* about himself, so very *goood* about himself on that special day.

One year later, when a little boy was born to the tailor and his wife, the tailor took his precious button and dangled it on a silken thread above the baby's bed.

As he grew, the little one began to play with that button, chew that button and suck that button. So the button wore out, wore out completely.

But as for the story of the tailor's button – why, that's a different matter. For if but one of you retells this tale to a friend or two, and one of your friends tells it on again, why, then we can be sure the story of the tailor's button will truly never wear out. No, not ever.

# Little River Turtle

Has your mother or father ever said to you that you can play out but mustn't go too far? Well, so it was with Little Turtle. His mother said to him, "You can go out of the river but don't go too far. No, no, no, don't go too far. Do you hear me?" She warned Little Turtle that if he went too far in the hot sun, his shell would crack… and then there'd be no more Little Turtle.

On the first day that I recall, Little Turtle swam up and out of the river and happened upon a patch of moist yellow sand. He drew a face in the sand and smiled back at the friend he'd made. Then, sploosh, splash, splosh, back into the river he went!

On the second day that I recall, Little Turtle swam up and out of the river and happened upon some nice juicy fronds of grass. He nibbled at them gently. They were delicious. Then, sploosh, splash, splosh, back into the river he went!

On the third day that I recall, Little Turtle swam up and out of the river and then his mouth dropped open… yes his mouth dropped open. He saw the most beautiful butterfly you could ever imagine, with iridescent blue wings that shimmered in the sunlight. When Little Turtle saw that butterfly his mouth dropped open and he forgot what his mother had said…

First, Little Turtle followed the butterfly through the short grass. When he travelled through that short grass and it tickled underneath his tummy, he felt like a clown in the circus and he giggled and giggled. Can you giggle too?

Well if the short grass was good — I tell you, the long grass was even better. For when Little Turtle travelled through the long grass, it stretched up all around him and he felt like a lion in the jungle and he roared and roared. Can you roar too?

Well if the long rough grass was good — I tell you, the little tiny pebbles were even better. For when Little Turtle travelled across the little tiny pebbles, he moved delicately from one to another and felt like a ballet dancer pirouetting across a stage.

Well if the little tiny pebbles were good — I tell you, the great big long smooth pebbles were even better. For when Little Turtle followed that butterfly across the great big long smooth pebbles, he slid right across their surface, and felt like an ice skater sliding across the surface of a frozen river.

A river…? Little Turtle realised he was a very long way from his river, but as the butterfly was still before him, he followed her faithfully out into the sands of the desert, until, "A-a-g-h-h!" Little Turtle felt a terrible pain. He remembered his mother's warning and knew his little body was drying out in the hot sun.

In desperation, Little Turtle looked around and on spying a small puddle underneath an overhanging clump of rocks, he hurried to that shelter as fast as he could, then plopped his soft underbelly into the puddle. The moisture began to seep up and under his shell. "Aaahh!" – that was better. But when Little Turtle looked out from his shady nook, he thought all was lost. He couldn't see his way home and there was nothing but dry sand and rocks in all directions. Little Turtle began to cry, "Aoow, aoow, aoow!" Poor Little Turtle, lost and alone, "Aoow, aoow, aoow!"

A few kilometres away, someone heard the sound. He pricked up his ears, cocked his head to one side and thought to himself, "What a beautiful song, I'd love to be able to sing that song." It was Coyote. He set out to find the source of the music, stealthily running towards it, his desire to learn the song deepening with every step. When he found Little Turtle he demanded to be taught the song.

"But I can't teach you this song," said Little Turtle, "because I'm not singing, I'm crying. Aoow, aoow, aoow!"

Coyote was not used to being crossed and he pawed the sand threateningly.

"Little Turtle," he snarled, "if you don't teach me that song, I'll snap you up in my mouth and run out into the open desert and drop you on your back, where you'll bake like a cake in the hot sun."

"But I can't teach you this song," said Little Turtle, "because I'm not singing, I'm crying. Aoow, aoow, aoow!"

Coyote continued to paw the ground and his eyes grew thin and mean and glinted in the sunlight.

"Little Turtle," he snapped, "if you don't teach me that song, I'll snap you up in my mouth and run out into the open desert and drop you onto a cactus. It'll be like acupuncture you haven't asked for."

"But I can't teach you this song," said Little Turtle, "because I'm not singing, I'm crying. Aoow, aoow, aoow!"

Coyote pawed the ground, glared out of his mean eyes and bared his long thin canines.

"Little Turtle," he spat, "if you don't teach me that song, I'll snap you up in my mouth and I'll… I'll… run to the nearest river and throw you in and you will drown." Little Turtle looked up at Coyote and his eyes smiled – well, just a little.

"But I can't teach you this song," he insisted, "because I'm not singing, I'm crying. Aoow, aoow, aoow!"

Snap! Coyote held Little Turtle firmly in his teeth and ran as fast as his legs would carry him. Across the desert, over the great big long smooth pebbles, over the little tiny pebbles, through the long grass and over the short grass. When he reached the river, Coyote threw Little Turtle high into the sky and down, down, down he fell into the water, sploosh, splash, splosh! "Oooh!" the cool water was delicious.

Little Turtle swam to the surface of the water and, lifting one flipper, he called out to Coyote on the bank, "Thank you, thank you, thank you."

Coyote slunk away, still practising the song. Indeed, generations of coyotes have continued to practise Little Turtle's song. For if you or I were to visit the desert today and the moon was high, we would undoubtedly see a coyote or two, their heads held high, singing that song, "Aoow, aoow, aoow!"

# The Rajah's Big Ears

Once, long ago, when the rulers of the lands of India were called Rajahs, there lived a Rajah who had big ears. When I say big, I mean they were massive, bigger than the biggest ears you or I have ever seen. They were so big that they would flap in the wind.

On windy days, the Rajah himself thought he would be blown away to the countries of his enemies, so on such days he would command that his most personal servants should tie his feet to the ground. No one, except his closest servants, knew about the Rajah's big ears, for he would hide his ears away under a huge hat that he wore whenever he was away from his bedchamber.

The Rajah was soon to be married and, in preparation for his wedding day, he needed to have his hair cut. So he went to a barber in the town. As the barber was about to remove the Rajah's hat, the Rajah said to him, "Now barber, when you remove my hat you will see that I have very large ears. I want you to keep this a secret. If I hear anything spoken about my ears, I will know who has been talking."

The barber, who had run his family business in the town for many years, replied, "Of course, Your Majesty, you can rely upon my silence over this matter."

The Rajah looked at the barber in the reflection of the mirror in front of him and frowned a dark and deadly frown. He said, "Barber, I'm pleased about this, for if I do hear anything spoken about my ears, I will ensure that you will lose your head!"

"Oh yes, I see," gulped the barber. "You can rely on me."

With that the Rajah slowly took off his hat and out flopped his humungous ears.

The barber, carefully avoiding the gigantic ears, cut the Rajah's hair beautifully. The Rajah was most pleased. When the barber had finished, he gently put the royal hat over the royal head and ears. Just as the Rajah was leaving, he turned and said, "Oh, and barber – please don't forget what we spoke about, will you?"

The trembling barber knew just what he meant.

☆ ☆ ☆

Have you ever been told a secret that makes you yearn to tell the whole world, a secret so interesting you become desperate to tell everyone? Well, the barber had this kind of a secret. He was desperate to tell someone about the Rajah's big ears.

When he went home, the barber went to see his wife, who was seated in front of her mirror, putting on large dangling earrings.

"Dear husband," she said. "Do you think these look too small for my ears?"

Without thinking what he was saying, the barber replied automatically, "Oh no, darling, not on you at all, but I'll tell you who they would look small on, that's the Rajah, because he has such large… ooooops!"

"Large what?" asked the barber's wife, half turning round as she attached her second earring.

"Oh fool, what am I saying?" thought the barber. "Do I want to lose my head?"

"Oh," he said. "Ah… um… large… large legs, yes, large legs. He's so tall, the earrings would not dangle low enough."

"Phew," thought the barber. "That was a close one."

His wife just frowned and looked up to God. How silly her husband was.

Then the barber went downstairs to where his two boys were playing with each other. One was sticking his tongue out and pulling his ears at the other. When the barber saw this, he suddenly said without thinking, "I should be careful if I was you, or you'll start looking like the Rajah."

"Why would I look like the Rajah, papa?" asked the boy.

"Because he's got big… ooooops."

And he slapped his hand over his mouth.

"What am I saying? Do I want to say 'bye bye' to my head!"

"Big what, papa?"

"Big children – he's got awfully big children."

"Phew," thought the barber. "That was another close shave."

☆ ☆ ☆

Things were getting difficult for the barber. He knew he would have to tell someone soon or the secret would just burst out. So he decided to walk out into the forest where no one ever went and he stood in front of a tree. He looked behind the tree, he looked to the sides of the tree and he looked all around him. He took a deep breath and said in a loud, clear voice, "The Rajah has big ears."

Then he said it again, this time in a high voice. Then he said it again in a low voice. Then he danced around the trees, singing that the Rajah has big ears.

Then he stopped, and with great relief walked off home.

☆ ☆ ☆

The next day some woodcutters went to the forest. They cut down all the trees where the barber had been and sold the wood to a musical instrument maker. She used the wood to make Indian instruments, including a stringed instrument called a sitar and many sets of drums called tabla. These instruments were sold to a band of musicians, who played them at important occasions.

The day of the Rajah's wedding came and all the townspeople were invited to a great feast after the ceremony. The Rajah and his new wife sat on thrones overlooking the guests. The barber was there with his family. He felt proud to have been invited and pleased to have kept the secret from everyone else in the town. Suddenly, a band of sitar and tabla players began to play. To the barber's dismay, he

heard the wooden instruments begin
to sing:

*The Rajah has big ears*
*The Rajah has big ears*
*Do you know what?*
*I know what*
*The Rajah has big ears.*

The Rajah sprang up
from his throne and bellowed,
"STOP, STOP, STOP! I heard
that."

The whispering crowd were hushed
into terrified silence.

The Rajah suddenly knew who must have revealed his secret and shouted at the
top of his voice, "BARBER!"

The barber stepped out from the throng of people, rubbing his hands and with
his head bowed. He was scared out of his life.

"Yes… gulp… Your, Your Majesty," he stuttered, terrified that he was about to
lose his head.

"I heard the words in that song and I know it could have been only you who has
disobeyed me and revealed the secret. I told you never to tell another person and
you have. For this you will lose your head – tonight!" said the Rajah.

"B, b, but Your Majesty, I didn't tell another person. I, I, I, told, I told… a tree,"
replied the barber, who was now shaking with fear.

There was a silence as the Rajah looked down at the barber with one of his
eyebrows cocked higher than the other.

Then, suddenly, a smile broke out on the Rajah's lips and slowly he began a long
and loud belly laugh, muttering, "He didn't tell a person, he told a tree. Oh, that's
funny. It is funny. He told a tree, not a person. Ha, ha, ha, ha! Oh, what am I
worrying about?" he continued. "So what if I've got big ears? Some people have
small feet, or big noses. We're all different and we always will be."

And with that, the Rajah pulled off his hat and shouted, "Friends and
townspeople, the Rajah has big ears. Let the music play."

And the band played on:

*The Rajah has big ears*
*The Rajah has big ears*
*I know he has*
*You know he has*
*The Rajah has big ears.*

# Anansi and Postman Snake

No one disliked work more than Anansi. While all the other animals were busy hunting for food and looking after their kind, Anansi would sit in the shade of the mango tree cooling himself with a large leaf and sipping ice-cold drinks.

Anansi liked to receive letters and could often be seen giggling at the ones he would get from his friends on other parts of the island. But he hated having to go to get them from the post office in the village. This would disturb his peace and interrupt his dozing.

One day, as Anansi lay on his back reading the papers, he saw Snake coming back from the post office. Snake moved with such smoothness and ease that Anasi called out to him. " Hey, Mr Snake, look how clean you slide along the road, so neat and so fast. You would make a wonderful postman."

Snake enjoyed the flattery and thanked Anansi for his words.

"Yes, indeed," said Anansi. "How would you like to become my postman and carry my letters and my newspapers to me every morning?"

"How much would you pay me, Anansi?" enquired Snake. "I wouldn't give up my time for nothing at all."

Anansi scratched his chin and said, "Snake, I know you like the taste of blood. You come over to my house at night and when you reach there you could bite me on the head and drink my blood. Of course, you mustn't bite too hard!"

Snake licked his lips at the prospect of a regular supper every night and so he agreed to become Anansi's postman.

Snake was up bright and early in the morning, bringing Anansi's mail. It was heavy work because Anansi was popular with animals from all over, and he had a very large sack of letters. Anansi made Snake work hard, sending him back to collect his papers, milk or other provisions. At the end of the day, Snake was well ready for his meal of Anansi's blood.

That night, Snake entered Anansi's house through the door Anansi had left open and gave him a bite on his head and drank his blood. It was a sharp bite; so sharp that Anansi was moody all the next day as the pain interrupted his leisure.

Anansi kept Snake busy again, running all around the village, slithering errands for him, but Anansi knew he could not stand another bite from Snake.

That evening, Anansi invited Rabbit over for dinner and at the end of the meal he invited Rabbit to sleep over. Anansi insisted that Rabbit should have his room and wanted to give up his bed for him. But Rabbit knew that Anansi was a trickster who was up to no good with this unusual 'generosity'. Rabbit challenged him, "Anansi, why are you doing this for me, giving up your room and your comfortable bed?"

My dear friend Rabbit," replied Anansi, "you are my dearest friend and for that you must have my comfortable bed. I shall be happy sleeping in the back room tonight."

But Rabbit was too wise and that night burrowed his way out of Anansi's house as soon as he could, before Snake arrived.

A little later, Snake turned up hungry for his blood. He had been working very hard all day for Anansi and now he wanted his refreshing reward. He thumped on the door with his tail shouting, "Anansi, let me in, it's the snake postman!"

There was no reply. In the darkness, Anansi waited for Rabbit to get up and let Snake in. Snake called again and again. Eventually, Anansi got out of bed in the pitch black and tiptoed into his room where he thought Rabbit was sleeping.

"Rabbit, brother Rabbit, could you open the door to let brother Snake in?"

When there was no reply, Anansi lit his lamp and saw the hole Rabbit had left by his departure – Rabbit had gone.

What was Anansi to do now? He liked having his letters delivered for him, but no way could he take another bite like that from Snake. Anansi started to cry out to Snake, saying how much his head hurt from the last bite and that he would have to go to the doctor.

Snake would hear none of it. He wanted blood. Snake began to grow angry and cried out, "Open the door Anansi, now – or I will go and bring a policeman!"

At that moment Anansi's eyes fell on a large black cooking pot standing on the stove. He grabbed the pot and put it on his head.

"Ready now, Snake", he called. "I'm sorry for keeping you but, alright, I'm ready now."

Anansi opened the door and put his head out into the darkness. Snake did not see the pot on Anasi's head because it was so dark. He was angry for being kept waiting and he bit as hard as he could. With a loud clang, Snake's teeth and gums hit the iron pot and he let out a pained yell that would have woken the animals on the other islands. He slithered off with bleeding gums and teeth and a pounding head.

The next day a message was sent to Anansi saying that Snake had to give up his job as a postman and was too ill to return for his wages.

Anansi was happy at this news. He lay back against the mango tree and smiled.